Thoughts Out of Season

R. W. Byrum

Table of Contents

1) New Year's Resolutions

In past years whenever someone asked me what my New Year's resolution had been I would reply that I had resolved not to make New Year's resolutions. In fact, I never used to observe New Years at all. I did not participate in the counting down to midnight and I did not toast the coming of the new year.

This year was a little different. I didn't celebrate. On the contrary, I went to bed almost an hour before midnight on New Year's Eve. What made this year different was that I made a New Year's resolution. I resolved to resume writing.

I have been writing on and off since 2000. For the first four years it was strictly a hobby for me. I spent that time writing fan fiction. Then in 2004 I abandoned fan fiction and started writing original material.

I found writing original fiction far more satisfying than writing fan fiction. I quickly found that I preferred building my own sandbox to playing in someone else's. When you write original fiction you have complete creative control which is something you do not have when you write fan fiction. Not to mention the fact that you can publish original fiction and perhaps earn money for your efforts which you cannot do with fan fiction.

As I already mentioned, my productivity was not consistent. Some days I would spend as much as sixteen hours writing while there were other days when I wouldn't write at all. There were times when I would give up altogether for a number of months, but I would always start up again. In twelve years I wrote three novels, about twenty short stories, a theological treatise and the memoirs of my experiences with cancer. These were the books I completed. There were a number of writing projects I began and never managed to complete.

During 2016 my writing alternated between periods of manic productivity and periods of complete inactivity. The last period of inactivity occurred near the end of the year. For about two or three weeks I did not write at all. My resolutions for 2017 were to write every day and to complete my unfinished writing projects.

During the last couple of weeks of 2016 I conceived of a new writing project. I decided to call this project *Thoughts Out of Season*. My conception for *Thoughts Out of Season* was that it would be a collection of short pieces of opinion and commentary. A kind of thought diary, if you will.

The topics would be whatever I was thinking about at the time and would be written in chronological order. The book would not be organized into chapters, rather each topic would stand alone and be both numbered and titled. The length of the topics would be determined by how much I have to write on the subject. There would be no minimum length and no maximum length. While the topics would be arranged chronologically, if I think of additional material for a given topic I would append the new material to the earlier topic rather than start a new topic. That way there would not be multiple topics written on the same subject, at least not within the same volume.

When the resulting manuscript reached 100,000 words I would publish it. This book would be the first in a series with subsequent thoughts recorded in future volumes. At least that was the original plan but as January flowed into February and I neared the 25,000 word mark I decided to publish the first volume when the manuscript reached 50,000 words.

The main impetus for this decision was the realization that my thoughts have become so dominated by the Trump Administration that I thought it better to publish those thoughts sooner rather than later.

Initially I had expected politics and current events to contribute only slightly to my thought processes. I had expected my thoughts to be dominated by personal issues and historical events as those are the things which have dominated my thought processes in the past.

Yesterday I made another slight revision to my plans for this manuscript. After publishing it I would make further thought entries into a new manuscript which I would title *Thoughts Out of Season, Volume II*. But whether this manuscript actually becomes published under that title would depend upon the success of the initial volume. If *Thoughts out of Season* proves successful, then I would go forward with plans to publish the new material as *Volume II*. If the initial volume does not sell well, then I would simply append the new material to the original manuscript and republish it as a second addition.

Success would mean a series of books each about 50,000 words long. Lack of success would result in a series of books each about 100,000 words long. Of course, if *Thoughts Out of Season* proves successful then it would remain my primary writing project. If it is not successful, then other projects would be moved forward as my principle writing projects while future contributions to the *Thoughts Out of Season* series would be relegated to secondary project status.

I have also decided to do something with *Thoughts Out of Season* that I had never done with my previously published books. I have decided to include a picture of myself on the back cover. While I have no intention of taking a new photograph of myself for this purpose, I have decided to use an existing recently taken photograph which represents how I actually look on a typical day.

I have always felt a sense of optimism at the beginning of the year. Each New Year's Day was a new beginning for me. This was especially true whenever New Years Day fell on a Sunday. Then the week, the month and the year all began on the same day. So, 2017 started especially propitiously, despite the fact that there was no real reason for such optimism and plenty of reasons for suspecting that the year would be a bad one. I have always found that optimism felt better than pessimism.

2) Celebrity Deaths

Celebrities die every year. Most of them after enjoying a long life and a distinguished career. Nevertheless, I have always felt a little sense of loss at their passing. As if a little piece of my own life had just disappeared. 2016 seemed to have had more than its share of celebrity deaths.

While the sense of loss is still real when the celebrity in question has attained an advanced age, such as William Christopher, Doris Roberts or Debbie Reynolds, or who had long since retired. It takes on more of the dimensions of tragedy when the celebrity dies suddenly and young, such as Anton Yelchin. Then you cannot help but wonder what they would have accomplished if they had lived longer. Then the sense of loss is a great deal deeper.

3) Glasses

I have worn glasses since I was six years old. I was born with hyperopia, farsightedness. Since my eyes focus beyond what I am looking at, I can see everything but I cannot see the fine details. So, no one realized that there was anything wrong with my eyesight until I started going to school. My first grade teacher realized I needed glasses when she noticed that I was squinting when looking at the blackboard.

People sometimes ask me why I don't switch to contact lenses. The main reason I did not make such a switch was because I do not easily tolerate having anything touching my eyeballs. In fact, until very recently the optometrists have not been able to screen me for glaucoma because they were not able to press the device to measure internal eye pressure against the outside of my eyeballs.

Another reason why I never switched to contact lenses was that I really didn't want to be bothered with the maintenance. Also, seeing a person drop a contact lens on the floor once was enough to convince me not to have them. When you need corrective lenses to see fine details the prospect of having to locate a clear piece of plastic with the unaided eye is quite unappealing.

Eyeglasses are not maintenance free, however. They need to be cleaned periodically. I should clean mine every day but I am far too lazy to do so. Usually I wait until the eye strain from peering through dirty lenses is enough to start bothering me before I bother to clean them.

Most of the dirt befouling my glasses are dust particles floating in the air. They are deposited on my glasses while walking around or even when just sitting down.

Sometimes things are splashed on my glasses. Whenever I have to walk out in the rain some of the rain drops find their way onto the lenses of my glasses. Sometimes liquids will be splashed up into my face. Naturally, some of that liquid will also find its way onto my glasses. But perhaps the worst thing to be deposited onto my glasses is snot.

Sometimes when I sneeze some of the snot will end up on my glasses. Most of the time these deposits will be on the outside of the lens but there have been times when the mucous was somehow deposited on the inside aspect of the lens.

I sometimes wonder how these mishaps occur. After all, the snot has to not only fly upwards to go from the opening of my nostril to my glasses but would also have to practically perform a U-turn. I usually attribute this strange phenomenon to electro-magnetic force. That seems to me to be the only way to account for this rather strange behavior. After all, electro-magnetic force is much stronger than either gravity or aerodynamics.

As staring through a lens partially coated in mucous is especially irritating, the deposition of snot on my glasses necessitates immediate cleaning.

My preferred method of cleaning my glasses is to use Windex and a paper towel. They make lens cleaner but it comes in such small containers that I usually use it up too quickly. Windex is much cheaper. Simply wiping my lenses with a soft cloth is not sufficient because the dirt coating my lenses is often greasy. Using a cloth will not remove the dirt, it will simply smear it across the lens. That's why I need a solvent, like Windex, to dissolve the grease adhering to the dirt and the lenses.

Still, it often takes several applications before I can clean the lenses sufficiently to relieve the eye strain. This is why specially formulated lens cleaner is so uneconomical for me. I go through a tube of it in a day or two.

Windex and a paper towel are not the recommended tools for cleaning glasses. Windex is too strong and paper towels are too abrasive. Optometrists and opticians advise using lens cleaner and a soft cloth. But Windex is better at removing grease as well as being significantly cheaper.

4) *Bones*

I have been watching *Bones* for about three and a half years now. I watch the show on Netflix rather than on broadcast television, so I don't get to see the show until about a year after it is first broadcast.

I really liked the show at first but I find it wearing thin on me the longer I watch it. The main reason for my growing disenchantment with the show is the character of Dr. Temperance Brennan as played by Emily Deschanel.

I don't really have an issue with Ms. Deschanel's performance, per se. She is simply portraying the character the way the directors and writers have conceived it. But after watching nine seasons of the show I find the personality of Dr. Brennan increasingly grating. She is arrogant, smug and conceited, character traits which are personality flaws that I usually associate with immaturity.

Instead of growing emotionally the character seems to be regressing. Experience should make her less arrogant, less smug and less conceited, but she seems to be growing more arrogant, more smug and more conceited as the seasons go by.

Dr. Brennan's character development reached a new low in the fourteenth episode of the ninth season when she becomes jealous of Dr. Saroyan being named "Outstanding Woman of Science" by a prestigious magazine. Rather than being happy for her friend and co-worker, Dr. Brennan was jealous, thus displaying the deep seated pettiness in her character. Dr. Brennan could not accept anyone else receiving an honor which she had not received because of her conceit that she was superior to everyone else.

During the thirteenth episode in the ninth season Dr. Brennan makes a comment that she is superior at interpreting x-rays than medical doctors. Unfortunately, the writers chose to reinforce this conceit rather than challenge it by having Dr. Brennan correctly diagnose an illness which the medical doctors had missed. How a forensic anthropologist can become better at making a medical diagnosis than a physician was something I could not understand. After all, how much experience with pathology would an anthropologist have? Especially one whose career involved examining victims of violent death rather than the progress of disease.

The discipline of physical anthropology involves identifying bones and bone fragments and rearticulating fragmented skeletons. It also involves recognizing physical differences in bones so that the anthropologist can determine the age, sex and race of the person from whom the bones derived. Physical anthropologists are also experts in identifying marks on bones to distinguish between tooth marks and tool marks and also to identify the type of tool used, its design and composition. That is why a physical anthropologist would be invaluable in identifying skeletal remains and perhaps also in determining cause and manner of death. However, I do not accept the supposition that a physical anthropologist would be superior to a medical doctor in diagnosing an disease.

Another aspect of Dr. Brennan's arrogance is that while she actually is superior to everyone else, that superiority is confined to a very narrow field. Outside of that field she is actually inferior to most other people and she doesn't seem to realize it. I find this to be the worst part of her character.

I contrast this to the character of Lt. Commander Data from *Star Trek: The Next Generation*. In the shows pilot Commander Riker asked Commander Data if he thought that he was superior. Data's answer was, "In many ways I am superior, but I would give all that up to be human." This answer reflected the character's belief that while he did enjoy superiority in some areas, when taken as a whole he regarded humans as his equals. Otherwise he would be a fool to want to be like them. Dr. Brennan regarded herself as superior to everyone else.

Despite my increasing disenchantment with Dr. Brennan I do intend to continue watching the television show. I'm just glad that the twelfth season will be the final one. The writers won't have much opportunity to allow her to devolve too much further.

As if the writers of *Bones* intentionally sought to reinforce my negative opinion of the character of Dr. Brennan, they actually had her stoop to a new low near the beginning of the twenty-second episode of the ninth season. When a body falls into the laps of a family of campers, the Jeffersonian is tasked with processing the body in situ. This is normally how the episodes begin with Dr. Brennan normally leading the forensics team.

However, in this episode Dr. Saroyan, the head of the forensics lab, suspects that Dr. Brennan is too biased to properly evaluate the evidence. Accordingly, she assigns Dr. Edison to head the team in Dr. Brennan's place. Cam calls Seely Booth and directs him to inform Dr. Brennan of her decision. Agent Booth disagrees with the decision but carries out his instructions nevertheless. However, Dr. Brennan shows up at the crime scene anyway. Her ego will not allow her to remain on the sidelines, not even after her superior has ordered her to remain in the lab.

In the real world, Dr. Brennan's blatant insubordination would be grounds for a formal reprimand if not termination. Yet in the show nothing happens to her. Just another example of the writers enabling and abetting the character's arrogance.

At the beginning of the twenty-fourth and final episode of the ninth season of *Bones*, Dr. Temperance Brennan's normal cold rationality is completely displaced by hot passion when Sealy Booth is brought into the emergency room with a gunshot wound to the chest. While this scene should have been a touching example of pathos, I found I could not sympathize with Dr. Brennan. Unfortunately, the character displayed the arrogant sense of entitlement that I have found increasingly irritating as the series moved forward.

When the nursing staff quite properly refused to allow her admittance into the trauma room, rather than recognize the professionalism of the hospital staff and acquiescing to their demands she attempts to brush past the nurse. She even goes so far as to call herself a doctor in her efforts to gain admission to a room which she has no right to enter. While Dr. Brennan calling herself a doctor was not technically a lie as she does have a PhD. However, in the context of a hospital emergency room she was implying that she possessed medical expertise which she did not have.

I have to admit that I did derive a great deal of satisfaction from the end of the episode. Dr. Brennan was arrested by the FBI because she refused to obey the doctor's orders and rushed in to see Seely Booth in his hospital room.

Season ten seems little changed from season nine. The character of Dr. Brennan hasn't improved but hasn't grown worse, either. I can't help but wonder if the fat guy found in the storm drain at the beginning of the third episode of the tenth season was based on Rush Limbaugh. The victim in that episode was described as a grotesquely obese right wing radio talk show host. Sure sounds like a Limbaugh surrogate.

My main complaint against *Bones*, besides the lack of character development in Dr. Brennan, has to do with the pacing of the show. The characters almost always manage to solve the crime and they almost always elicit a confession from the perpetrator at the end of the show. I don't have a problem with either, it's just that the confessions always seem to come to easily at the end.

This is because the show's writers waste too much time on the characters' personal issues and often spend too much time on the investigation itself leaving themselves without enough time to properly confront the perpetrator with the evidence of their guilt.

17

Then again, I often wonder why the writers feel it necessary for the perpetrator to freely confess at the end of each show. In the real world perpetrators rarely confess no matter how damning the evidence against them. This is due to the fact that it is much easier to exclude evidence at trial than it is to exclude a confession. Isn't providing the proof of the perpetrator's guilt enough? Isn't having the perpetrator confessing merely gilding the lily?

5) Success and the Literary Establishment

The overall pattern of my life has been one of repeated failures. I joined the army but was discharged before completing basic training. I attended the University of Maryland but dropped out before earning a degree. My marriage ended in divorce after only three years. I joined the United States Postal Service but was fired before the end of my probationary period. From all of these failures I learned how to deal with failure. I also learned not to take success for granted.

I have to admit that despite my track record when I started writing original fiction I dreamed of success. I doubt that anyone seriously undertakes anything without first imagining that they would be successful and imagining what that success would entail.

What would literary success entail? Most people imaging that literary success would be having one's book published by a major publishing house and having that book become an international best seller. Success would mean seeing their book in the bookstores and on the library shelves. In this regard I was no different than most people.

That was why I followed the usual formula for literary success. I wrote a novel and submitted it to literary agents. When none of the queried agencies showed interest in representing me, I began to submit my manuscript to publishers who did not require submissions to be sent by an agent.

When that didn't work, I assumed that the manuscript was unacceptable. Therefore, I re-wrote the book and started all over again, submitting it first to literary agents and then to publishing houses. When that didn't work I tried writing a second novel. I also wrote short fiction and submitted the stories to every magazine in the country who might have even the slightest interest in publishing them. But every magazine to which I submitted a story sent me a rejection notice and agents and publishers showed no more interest in my second novel than they did in my first.

The literary establishment had rejected me. Like everyone else, I had believed that membership in the literary establishment was a prerequisite for literary success. Eleven years of failing to break into publishing caused me to re-evaluate what I was doing. I started to question the caliber of my writing and then I inevitably came to question whether I even possessed sufficient talent to become a successful author. I seriously considered quitting. After all, if I couldn't be successful with my writing what was the point of even doing it?

I would look over books that had been published and I honestly could not see why the published books were better than my unpublished manuscripts. I even compared my writing to the best writers in the field and I still did not believe that my writing was inherently inferior. Maybe that was arrogance but it was how I honestly thought. A writer who does not think his own writing is good has no business trying to publish it.

Then I came to believe that the problem wasn't with myself or with my writing but was caused by the very nature of literary establishment itself. What is the literary establishment? It is the conglomeration of the businesses and individuals who produce and promote works of fiction.

The literary establishment includes not only the publishing houses but also the bookstore chains, the literary agencies, the organizations that administer literary awards and prizes, literary critics and published authors.

Whether or not any given novel was published had nothing to do with the manuscript's literary merits and everything to do with its marketability. The literary establishment would publish and promote anything which they believed they could sell to the public, regardless of its quality. Conversely, the literary establishment would refuse to publish or promote any book which did not promise a handsome profit regardless of how well written or conceived it may be.

Are we to believe that Dan Brown suddenly became a brilliant author with his fourth book? Hardly. It just happened that he hit upon a formula which resonated with the reading public. *The Da Vinci Code* was one of the bestselling books of all time, but it could hardly be described as one of the best conceived or the best written.

The defining characteristic of the literary establishment is exclusivity. Because of this the literary establishment will admit only a very few number of authors into its ranks every year and it is this exclusivity that guaranteed that I would never be admitted into the literary establishment. Couple this with the widespread belief that membership in the literary establishment was a prerequisite for literary success and you can see why I came to believe that literary success would be forever beyond my reach. After all, were there any successful authors who were not a member of the literary establishment? I couldn't think of any.

So, when I concluded that I would never be admitted into the literary establishment, I also concluded that I would never find literary success. Yet I continued to write nevertheless. Why? Because I decided that literary success was no longer a goal of mine.

Instead my goal would be to find self-fulfillment through my writing. I stopped worrying about marketability or even caring whether I would ever find an audience for my work. All of my writing effectively became acts of literary masturbation. Rather than trying vainly to please others, I would seek to please myself. I wrote exactly what I wanted to write, exactly how I wanted to write it. I stopped worrying about other peoples' opinions. I stopped worrying about whether my work was ever reviewed or what those who did review it would say. I would no longer bother to market my work. I would simply self publish it and if it sold so much the better and if it didn't, so what?

Success, to me, no longer had anything to do with royalties and book sales. Success entailed writing my thoughts down and offering them up to the world. With each manuscript that I completed and published I became more fulfilled and therefore, more successful. And that is a type of success that no one can ever deprive me of.

6) The Election of 2016

The election of 2016 was certainly one of the more interesting elections in recent memory. Both of the major parties devolved into their lowest common denominators and nominated standard bearers who were the perfect personifications of their respective parties. I wasn't surprised that one party would cater to their extremes at the expense of their center, but I was surprised that both parties did it at the same time. Usually one party has sense enough to promote a more moderate candidate and thereby win the election. Of course, a moderate President does make it harder for the extremists to promote their agenda.

But, this election was different. Thus the democrats nominated an arrogant, narcissistic, northeastern liberal career politician while the republicans chose an arrogant, narcissistic, billionaire. Neither candidate was able to appeal to enough of the electorate to garner a majority of the votes, though Hillary Clinton did earn more than Donald Trump. Trump's victory was due to quirks in the electoral college and even so, he was barely able to pull off the win.

The strangest part about this election was the lack of support Trump's candidacy had within the Republican Party itself. Party leaders were calling on Trump to drop out of the race even after he secured the party's nomination. Prominent Republicans such as Brent Scowcroft, Condoleezza Rice and Paul Wolfowitz actually publicly favored Hilary Clinton over Trump.

After the election Wolfowitz said that he did not vote for Clinton despite his stated intention before the election to do so. Wolfowitz may not have been able to force himself to vote for Clinton but that certainly does not mean that he voted for Trump. I think it most likely that he voted Libertarian in the election. George Will, a lifelong Republican, abandoned the GOP when Trump won the party's nomination. Even he admitted that Clinton was a better candidate which must have been a very painful admission for him.

Now that the republicans have a majority in both the House and the Senate, Donald Trump's inauguration on January 20th will give the Republican Party firm control over the entire federal government.

Will the Republicans use this power wisely? If recent history is any indication, then the answer is a resounding 'no'. Every time the Republicans gain control of the House, the Senate and the White House, they have invariably pushed through an agenda obviously designed to promote the interests of big business. Or at least, an agenda that the managers of major corporations believed to be in their best interests.

This agenda proved to be disastrous, not only for the country as a whole but for the very businesses that were supposed to benefit most from that agenda. Witness both the savings and loan disaster in the 1980's and the investment banking crisis of 2008. Time will only tell which industry the Republicans destroy with deregulation this time around.

With the election of Donald Trump to the White House the Republican Party has completed its transformation from the Grand Old Party to the Grand Order of Plutocrats.

7) Conservatism and the Republican Party

Yesterday I read two opinion pieces analyzing Donald Trump. One was by noted conservative commentator George Will. The other was by Michael Gambon. Neither man gave a very flattering appraisal of the President-elect. Mr. Gambon declared that Donald Trump would either be completely incompetent or trigger a constitutional crisis. Mr. Will characterized Trump's election as the "nadir of conservatism".

While I am not familiar with Michael Gambon, I am quite familiar with George Will. I have seen him debate politics on Agronsky and Company and I have occasionally read his syndicated column. I have always had the utmost respect for George Will and have always taken his opinion very seriously, even when I disagreed with it. I was greatly impressed with his poise, his erudition and his beautifully crafted prose. He was a man I could respect even while disagreeing with him.

I am not a conservative myself, so I have come largely to rely upon Mr. Will's articles to inform me of conservative ideology and the conservative position on many issues. I much prefer to rely upon an intellectual of George Will's standing to relying on a demagogue like Rush Limbaugh. Mr. Will's analysis seems deep and penetrating whereas Mr. Limbaugh's analysis never runs any deeper than whether a 'D' or an 'R' appears after a politician's name in the newspapers.

The Republican Party began its life as the abolitionist party. Its first presidential candidate was John C. Fremont in 1856. For the first sixty years of its existence the Republican Party was actually the progressive party, the Democrats were the traditional conservatives. The switch in the party's ideology from progressivism to conservatism occurred during the presidency of William Howard Taft.

Theodore Roosevelt was so incensed by this that he challenged Taft for the Republican nomination in 1912 and when that bid failed, ran as a third party candidate in the general election. This resulted in the victory of a progressive Democrat, Woodrow Wilson. Naturally, under Wilson's leadership the Democratic Party began its transformation from the conservative party to the liberal party.

Naturally, this transformation did not happen all at once nor did it occur at the same rate in every part of the country. The liberalization of the Democratic Party occurred first in the northeast and progressed there faster than in other parts of the country. The Democrats of the south remained conservative well into the twentieth century. In fact, it wasn't until the Reagan years in the 1980s that southern conservatives left the Democratic Party and became Republicans.

Now, just a little over a hundred years after the transition, the Republican Party has been so successful at branding itself as the conservative party that no one seriously challenges the appropriateness of the label.

Conservatism is the belief that the traditional ways of thinking and doing things were better and therefore should be preserved. Thus conservatives are suspicious of change and always seek to oppose it. Because of its nature, conservatism is tied to time and place. Because of differences in cultural values the conservatives in one country may be very different from the conservatives in another. Just consider what it means to be a conservative in a country like Saudi Arabia. Similarly, because of changes that have occurred over time a man who would be considered conservative by the standards of today may well have been considered a progressive, even a radical, by the standards of the past.

Our own so-called "Revolutionary War" wasn't a true revolution at all. True revolutions seek to overthrow the established government and replace it with something else. By their very nature revolutions are exercises in progressivism. The French Revolution was an excellent example. It replaced the monarchy with a republic.

The American Revolution, in contrast, was actually an exercise in conservatism. That was precisely why it was not a true revolution. It did not seek to replace the government but rather was aimed at winning the independence of the American colonies. Thus, it was properly a war for independence and British historians properly identify it as such.

The revolution was touched off by acts of Parliament which sought to change the fundamental relationship between the colonies and the mother country and directly threatened to change how the colonies were governed.

The leaders of the colonies saw independence as the only way of preventing those changes. Thus the Revolution was not aimed at changing the way the colonies were governed, which is always the goal of a true revolution, but at preserving the traditional way of governing them. Even the Declaration of Independence was an accusation against the crown of violating the traditional English principles of government.

American conservatism today seeks to promote and preserve the ideology of Thomas Jefferson. Jefferson firmly believed that the government which governed best was the one which governed least. Therefore, the government should not be any larger than absolutely necessary to fulfill its obligations under the Constitution. The chief advantage of such a small government was that it would only require a small tax structure to support it. One of the issues which touched off the American Revolution was attempts by the British Parliament through taxation to get the American colonies to help pay for British imperialism.

American conservatives couple Jeffersonian theories of government with complete faith in free market capitalism. Conservatives believe that free market capitalism is the best vehicle for producing and distributing wealth and they are deeply suspicious of any other method. They see Democratic policies of wealth redistribution as wasteful and ultimately corrupting.

The goals of American liberalism are really no different than the goals of American conservatism. Both philosophies seek to promote personal freedom and the welfare of the people. What they differ on are the nature of the policies best designed to achieve these goals.

Conservatives believe that only effective way to promote the welfare of the people is to promote economic prosperity. They see the two greatest threats to that prosperity as taxation and government regulation. They also believe that the best way to promote personal freedom to keep the government as small and unobtrusive as possible. Government should largely be passive and keep out of the way of the people. They believe that people can best solve their own problems without government interference.

Liberals, on the other hand, believe that the problems of the people are often far too great for them to handle on their own. Thus, government must be proactive in helping the people overcome their problems. Obviously, to fulfill this expectation government must be both large and intrusive. Furthermore, such a government would require a substantial tax structure to support it.

While American conservatism certainly does have a natural tendency to promote business interests and by extension the interests of the wealthy, this does not necessarily mean that American conservatism seeks to promote the interests of business and the wealthy over the interests of the people. Though this has long been claimed by the Democrats.

Conservatives have long preached that through entrepreneurship, diligence and perseverance the poor can join the ranks of the wealthy. But only as long as they are not hampered by taxation and government regulation. Conservatives have always argued that it was principally government regulation which hindered social mobility rather than lack of opportunity.

The closing decades of the twentieth century and the opening decades of the twenty-first century have seen the ideology of the Republican Party shift away from its traditional conservatism to a more plutocratic ideology masquerading as conservatism. The complete identification of the Republican Party with conservatism in the public mind guaranteed that the electorate would not notice the change.

This substitution of plutocracy for conservatism had obviously been going on for quite some time before it became glaringly obvious in 2008. I strongly suspect that this substitution began during the presidency of Ronald Reagan. As I have already said, I am no conservative.

However, I have a very hard time reconciling the Reagan Administration's tripling of the national debt in just eight years with conservative ideology.

2008 brought with it the bursting of the housing bubble and the near collapse of the investment banking structure of the United States. The Bush Administration responded with the Emergency Economic Stabilization Act. A federal law which authorized the Treasury Department to bailout the investment banks. In passing this law the Republicans abandoned any pretense to conservative values. By bailing out the investment banks the Republicans were blatantly engaging in corporate welfare. There is absolutely nothing conservative about using tax money to prop-up private financial institutions. The Emergency Economic Stabilization Act was the triumph of plutocracy over conservatism.

If any serious doubts remained about the conversion of the Republican Party from the conservative party to the plutocratic party, the nomination and election of Donald Trump should have removed them.

In the past men like Trump were content to sit in the background and play the power behind the throne, pulling the strings of the politicians they patronized. But Trump's ego does not permit him to play the traditional role. He can't just manipulate the occupant of the throne, he must be the occupant of the throne. His ego would permit no less.

8) Driving Habits

There is no venue better for displaying the common propensity for human beings to be selfish and stupid than the morning and afternoon commutes. While I can certainly understand the desire to minimize one's daily commute, I do what I can to minimize my own. However,

I never put life and limb on the line for the sake of shaving a few seconds off of my time.

Some people seem to believe that it is okay for them to run through a red light without stopping if they don't see anybody in the intersection as they are approaching the light. In areas of Maryland near the District of Columbia running the red lights was so common that nobody dared to proceed when their own traffic light first turned green. They would wait at least thirty seconds to assure themselves that they would not be t-boned by some idiot running the red light on the cross street.

This habit of waiting doesn't always prevent accidents. I've personally seen close calls when a car nearly was hit in the intersection even when delaying their entrance into the intersection until nearly a minute after the light had turned green.

Here in Chambersburg things haven't gotten that bad yet. Blatantly running red lights here is rare. But I have witnessed habits that are potentially dangerous as well as annoying. Like many states, Pennsylvania allows right turns on red and the rules for making such turns are the same in Pennsylvania as they are in other states. The driver is required to come to a complete stop, signal his intention to turn and then wait to execute his turn when he can do so safely.

I have seen many Pennsylvania drivers violate these rules. Sometimes they don't bother to signal that they are making a turn. Most of the time the violators fail to come to a stop before turning. They simply barrel into the intersection just as if they had a green light. Once when I was making a left turn on a green arrow I almost had a collusion with a car who was making a right turn on a red light. He didn't stop at the light as the law required.

Naturally, turning right on red does not give the driver executing such a turn the right of way. On the contrary, drivers executing a right turn on red are only allowed to do so when there is no other traffic. They must yield not only to those already in the roadway but also to those who are turning on a green light or a green arrow. I have found that many drivers mistakenly think that turning right on red confers on them the right of way so they fail to yield to those making turns who should have precedence over them.

Another law commonly violated by the impatient is the Boulevard Law. This is the law that requires drivers to stop before enter the street, even when there is no stop sign or traffic signal. I can't even count the number of times I have seen drivers pull into the street from a parking lot without stopping first. Usually this happens because the offending driver knows that if he stops as the law requires he will have to wait to enter the street. By breaking the law the offending driver saves himself a few seconds.

I find that one of the most annoying experiences is watching another driver pull out into the street without stopping, presumably because he was in such a God-awful hurry that he could not tolerate to wait the five seconds for me to pass him before pulling out, just to have him drive slowly on the road, often driving significantly below the speed limit.

Such experiences led me to an interesting conclusion about drivers with bad driving habits. Most of what they do is not driven by impatience but by ego. By pulling out in front of me they weren't necessarily trying to save themselves a few seconds of time, they were asserting their dominance over me.

I find that a better explanation for aggressive driving than the prevailing belief that it is always driven by impatience. It also better explains road rage. Road rage incidents can't really be explained as frustrated impatience but they can be explained as frustrated attempts at asserting dominance. After all, why would impatience lead to violence? The assertion of dominance certainly can lead to violence. In fact, the resort to violence is the logical final step in asserting dominance.

I believe that bad driving habits are born out of the culture of competition. Through aggressive driving people are competing against their fellow drivers. By passing every other car on the road they are "beating" them in the race of life.

Consider the Amish. Their religious beliefs completely preclude them from participating in the culture of competition. Of course, driving a horse and buggy does pretty much eliminate any opportunity for aggressive driving which probably has a lot to do with the fact that they drive horses and buggies rather than cars.

I often wonder just how many aggressive drivers are NASCAR fans. How many of them are trying to live the fantasy of being a stock car racer. Some people certainly drive during the morning rush hour as though they were racing at Talladega. And just as some drivers inevitably crash as Talladega, so do some of the more aggressive drivers on the interstates.

9) Taiwan

The official name of Taiwan is the Republic of China. This reflects the fact that the government in Taipei claims to be the legitimate government of all of China and is currently in exile on the island of Taiwan. When Chiang Kai Shek lost the Chinese Civil War to Mao Tse Tung's communists forces in 1949, he fled to the island of Taiwan which had just recently been returned to China by Japan. At the time Chairman Mao did not have the naval forces necessary to pursue Chiang Kai Shek to Taiwan.

When Chairman Mao proclaimed the People's Republic of China in 1949, only the Soviet Union and its satellites recognized it as the legitimate government of

China. The United States and its allies continued to recognized Chiang Kai Shek's government in Taipei. Even China's permanent seat on the United Nations Security Council was held by the Taipei government. Mainland China was not even admitted to the United Nations.

This situation continued for decades. With economic and military backing from the United States, Taiwan was able to remain effectively independent of the People's Republic of China. Independent in everything but name. The Taipei government has never declared its formal independence from China, they continue to maintain that they are the legitimate government of China in exile.

Things started to change in 1972 when Richard Nixon and Henry Kissinger visited Chairman Mao in Beijing. At this historic summit began a process that eventually led by the end of the decade to the United States formally transferring its recognition from the Taipei government to the Beijing government.

This transference led to the opening of the American embassy in Beijing and the Chinese embassy in Washington and the closing of the American embassy in Taipei. In fact, the United States government will not meet or even talk with the President of the Republic of China. This despite the fact that America still gives Taiwan substantial military aid.

Taiwan's seats in the United Nations were transferred to China as most of the rest of the world followed Washington's lead in recognizing the Beijing government as the rightful government of China.

Prior to 1979, a "Made in China" label meant that the article had been manufactured in Taiwan. Since 1979, all "Made in China" labels refer to the People's Republic of China. Anything imported from Taiwan today bears the label, "Made in Taiwan."

So, when President Elect Donald Trump accepted a congratulatory telephone call from Tsai Ing-wen, the

President of Taiwan, he was breaking with 37 years of protocol. The United States government has had no official dealings with Taiwan since 1979. The responsible thing would have been to refuse the call as receiving official congratulations from the President of Taiwan could be seen in Beijing as an indication that America might formally recognize the independence of Taiwan.

The People's Republic of China has always regarded Taiwan as a province of China and an integral part of their country. They regard Taiwan as a province in rebellion. The People's Republic of China even has a governor for Taiwan, though obviously he lives on the mainland and has no influence in Taiwan.

The government of mainland China has repeatedly warned that if Taiwan should formally declare its independence that the People's Republic would immediately invade the island. So far the Taipei government has not seen fit to test that threat. But if Trump does anything to encourage them, either wittingly or unwittingly, they just might decide that de facto independence is not enough.

10) "War is Hell"

Perhaps the most famous saying of William Tecumseh Sherman was "War is hell." Quoted like that out of context made the general seem like a callous bastard who was completely dismissing the horrors of armed conflict. But the quote as it is most often repeated is incomplete. The complete version ran something like this: "I am tired and sick of war. Its glory is all moonshine. It is only those who have neither fired a shot nor heard the shrieks and groans of the wounded who cry aloud for blood, for vengeance, for desolation. War is hell."

I have always felt safer when the leaders of powerful nations were combat veterans. I believe men who had experienced the horrors of war firsthand would not be so quick to resort to war to solve the nation's problems. That was why I really did not fear nuclear war growing up. Leonid Brezhnev experienced combat as a commissar during World War II. I believe that after living through such destruction that he would not be the man to launch a pre-emptive nuclear strike.

The leaders who made me nervous were the ones who had never seen combat and were advised largely by other men who had never seen combat, either. Especially when such men maintained a macho self image. Such chairborne rangers and armchair warriors were much more apt to start wars.

11) The Importance of a Positive Outlook

I used to be the overnight cashier at a gas station. I worked seven days a week which made my income much higher than my nominal rate of pay would suggest. My shift lasted from 10 p.m. until 6 a.m. Most of the customers I served were locals though the gas station certainly got its share of travelers from the nearby interstate.

I would see most of the locals at the same time every morning. Most of them came in between 5:00 a.m. and 6:00 a.m. Naturally, during the week they would be on their way to work. When they came to my gas station they would wear completely blank expressions on their faces, their movements were hesitant and jerky, and their speech was wooden. Despite looking completely healthy these customers behaved with all the animation of extras from a zombie movie.

One thing that struck me was seeing these same customers during hunting or fishing season. They would arrive even earlier than they would when going to work, often two or three hours earlier. Yet, when on their way to hunt or fish they would be lively and alert, as bright-eyed and bushy-tailed as anyone I had ever met.

The secret to the difference was state of mind. Going hunting or fishing imbued them with a positive outlook that no job could have given them.

12) President Elect Donald Trump

It is truly amazing. Donald Trump hasn't even been inaugurated yet he is already demonstrating his unfitness for office. He is requiring all of the 'political' ambassadors, obviously meaning those appointed by President Obama, to resign their offices by January 20th. This is completely unprecedented.

While it is to be expected that he will replace ambassadors with people of his own choosing, that is part of the nature of the game. Normally the incoming President waits at least until he is actually inaugurated before demanding resignations. Normally, they wait until they have appointed replacements and had those appointments confirmed by the Senate before removing people from office.

The appointment and confirmation process normally takes months. So Trump will deprive America of ambassadors to a number of important countries for the time it will take to appoint and confirm their replacements. This is terribly irresponsible to say the least and it might even be calculated.

Trump is effectively creating a crisis gratuitously. Doubtlessly, he will use the need to replace the ambassadors as expeditiously as possible in order to ram his appointments through the Senate. Sadly enough, the Republican Party will probably let him get away with this.

America will survive the Trump administration, but I am not so sure that the Republican Party will.

13) Love and Romance

I haven't experienced much of either love or romance in my life. There were a variety of reasons for this and if any fault has to be assigned for this lacking that fault must be laid firmly at my own feet.

The first and by far most important contributing factor to the lack of romance in my life was my own rather unsocial disposition. I have never been a people person. Normally, I have always kept to myself. I have never gone out of my way to meet people. Naturally, a disposition that rendered you unwilling to socialize was a decided handicap in finding romance.

This was not to say that I have been completely anti-social. I didn't refuse to talk to people when they talked to me, it's just that I was not the one who initiated such conversations. On rare occasions I have enjoyed some rather interesting conversations, but those experiences were not enough to overcome my basic disposition. For every witty conversationalist I have ever met I have encountered at least half a dozen ignorant dolts.

The second contributing factor was my physical appearance. While I was not especially ugly when I was young, I never regarded myself as especially handsome, either. I was not the type of guy that teenage girls or young women drooled over. Added to my rather plain appearance was the fact that I dressed plainly and was completely unconcerned with my personal grooming. I did not have a handsome face, a glib tongue, an outgoing personality, an athletic physique or even a rudimentary sense of fashion. There just was nothing really going for me.

Age has not improved me. I still dress in the same uninspired way I dressed in high school. I'm still just as indifferent to personal grooming. The fact that I am now going bald doesn't bother me in the least. On the contrary, I often think it rates as an improvement.

Naturally, the cancer has not improved my appearance, either. I now have both a rather pronounced surgical scar on the neck and mild lymphedema which gives my neck a swollen appearance. The weight loss which accompanied the cancer and the loss of almost all of my teeth have resulted in my face looking sunken. False teeth would serve no useful purpose for me and I refuse to be fitted with them for purely esthetic reasons.

The third factor leading to the lack of romance in my life was my due to my own attitudes about dating. Unlike most other people, I never dated just to have fun. Sexual attraction by itself was never sufficient motivation for me to ask anyone out on a date. This was because I refused to treat a date as an isolated event. I always regarded a date as a stepping stone to a lifelong relationship. Because of this I would never ask any woman out on a date unless I regarded her as a potential lifelong partner. If I knew that I wasn't interested in spending the rest of my life with a woman, I wouldn't bother to ask her out on a date. I regarded doing so as a complete waste of time.

Naturally, this meant that I was not a big fan of casual sex. I would never take a woman to bed with me unless I felt that I wanted to marry her and spend the rest of my life with her. If I was not willing to make such a complete commitment to her then I would regard engaging in sexual acts with her as a form of usury.

Naturally, I would never even consider the possibility of patronizing prostitutes, not even in locations where the world's oldest profession was perfectly legal. I didn't believe that paying for the privilege made casual sex any more usurious. Furthermore, I found that treating sex

37

as a business transaction fundamentally cheapened it. I felt that sharing sexual pleasure should bind oneself emotionally to one's partner. Otherwise, sex was just another biological function like defecating.

I never admired characters like Casanova or Don Juan. I never saw them as romantic figures. Instead, I had always conceived of them as selfish bastards who used women for their own pleasure and then cast them aside to move on to their next 'conquest'. Rather than seeing that behavior as romantic, I always thought of it as childish. The fact that there were women who emulated this behavior did not make it any more mature to me. Rather, I thought it was sad that some women chose to emulate the worst behavior in men and then congratulate themselves on being 'liberated'.

So, I never made it my practice to troll bars and nightclubs for vulnerable women to victimize in 'one night stands'. In fact, I never frequented either type of establishment. The only places I would go where I could meet other people were school and work and neither place seemed a particularly fertile venue for meeting my soul mate.

Why not? For the simple reason that the vast majority of the women whom I met at work or at school were not the type of women I would choose to date. This was the fourth factor leading to the lack of romance in my life. If I could not meet the woman who was perfect for me, I was unwilling to date women who were less than perfect simply because they were more available.

I have a pet theory that many relationships fail because people entered into them by accepting a second rate partner rather than waiting for the person they really wanted. This theory was based more on vague impressions rather than any statistical knowledge, so it was more likely to be wrong than right. However, it did explain my own mindset and why I would not settle for anyone who did not possess every characteristic I was looking for in a potential partner.

What am I looking for? I still carry the fantasy of perhaps fathering my own child, so ideally I would want a woman who was still young enough to bear children. This was not an absolute requirement, however. I would not refuse a woman solely on the basis of her age. That would be terribly hypocritical of me considering that I am now 51. Still, there are enough women willing to marry older men that it is not completely out of the realm of possibility.

I am definitely looking for a East Asian woman. That is not negotiable. I have such a strong attraction for East Asian women that I do not think that I would be completely happy with a woman who was not of East Asian descent. Why this is I do not know. The closest to an explanation I can give is the fact that I regard the epicanthic fold as the most beautiful feature a woman can have. I don't really understand the fad for Korean women to have theirs surgically removed. Seems to me that this robs them of much of their beauty.

That is not to say that I haven't approached women who were not East Asian. I have. In fact, I have even dated one. But that was at a time when I was willing to settle for less than my ideal. I would not currently even consider dating a woman who was not an East Asian.

I have certain mild fetishes. Nothing really perverse, I just find women more attractive when they wear certain articles of clothing, some of which aren't even usually considered particularly sexy.

Boots are my number one fetish. I will look at a woman wearing boots who would not otherwise attract my attention at all. I am especially fond of boots made of black or brown leather but I don't particularly care for suede. I much prefer boots that rise to a woman's knee or even higher, though there is a decided cultural bias against boots that rise much above the knee. Pity really as I've always found those types the most attractive.

The type of heel doesn't matter to me at all. High heels don't really appeal to me per se. My attraction for boots lies mainly in the way the shanks of the boots look on a woman's legs.

I don't care whether a woman wears pants, a skirt or tights with her boots provided that she tucks the legs of her pants into the shanks of her boots. That way I can actually see the boots. I especially like it when the color of a woman's clothes offers a high contrast to the color of her boots.

I suppose I should call my fetish a leather fetish rather than a boot fetish because it does include leather garments besides boots. I have always found leather gloves and leather belts equally fascinating. There are limits to my fascination with leather, however. I have never cared much for either leather pants or leather skirts and leather coats and jackets have never especially attracted my attention, either.

I do like trench coats, but trench coats made of cloth rather than leather. What I like about trench coats is that the waist is often gathered with a belt. I really like the way the coat looks on a woman with the waist gathered by a belt, especially if the belt is made of black leather and the coat is light enough in color to offer a high enough contrast to make the belt stand out.

I prefer the look of one piece bathing suits over the look of bikinis. This is because in general I usually find that less is more when it comes to nudity. I find one piece bathing suits more attractive because they cover up more of a woman's body while still emphasizing her figure. I find that bikinis simply reveal too much.

My strange preference for clothing that covers while still emphasizing the figure is the reason why I find a woman dressed in a jump suit a good deal more provocative than the same woman would be while scantily clad. Again, I especially like it when a woman wears a belt over her jumpsuit to gather the waist. This is because the belt helps the jumpsuit emphasize her figure.

On the whole I much prefer casual clothing to formal attire. I have always found jeans and a t-shirt a great deal more attractive than an evening gown. I think it just fits in with my utilitarian tastes. Dresses never really did much for me. Not even dresses expressly designed to be sexy.

I think the ultimate fantasy would be for me to meet an East Asian woman wearing a trench coat with the waist gathered by a leather belt who was also wearing boots, leather gloves and a jumpsuit over a one piece bathing suit. She would come to me and immediately sweep me off my feet. Even in my fantasies my non-social disposition prevents me from making the first move.

I often fantasize about going to bed with a woman I have just met. This might seem like a contradiction but it really is not. While I don't believe in casual sex I do believe in love at first sight.

Height is not an issue for me. East Asian women tend to be on the short side anyway. I am also quite liberal when it comes to weight but even there I do have my limits. I would not date a woman who looks like the fat lady from a circus side show. But that does not mean that I would necessarily reject a woman for being overweight. East Asian culture emphasizes thinness so much that many East Asian woman regard themselves as overweight whom I would regard as normal or even underweight.

I have tried my hand at online dating. In fact, I met my ex-wife that way. But besides my failed marriage my efforts at online dating all failed. During my last foray into online dating I became involved with a con-artist who wanted to involve me in a money laundering scheme. It's just too easy for people to misrepresent themselves online, either intentionally or unintentionally.

Despite my negative experiences I am still romantic enough to believe that I still have a chance at finding true love, no matter how slight that chance might be. In fact, my whole purpose of writing this section is the hope that it might somehow lead to me meeting the woman of my dreams.

14) Editing

I hate editing. It is the one part of the process of writing and publishing books which I truly despise. I would prefer to do just about anything else rather than edit what I have written.

That's why I always procrastinate when it comes time to edit my manuscripts and when I do get around to editing it always seems to take me forever to get it done. Case in point was my last novel. I think it actually took me longer to edit the damn thing than it took to write it in the first place.

I would gladly hire someone else to do it if I could afford to do so. Unfortunately, even a simple line edit costs between $3000 and $4000 for a manuscript the length of a full-sized novel. So, until I either win the lottery or my books begin providing more substantial royalties, it looks like I'll be performing my own editing.

One problem with self-editing is that you already know exactly what you were trying to say. So, what you write always makes sense to you even when it doesn't make sense to anyone else.

Another problem is that it is much harder to catch your own errors than it is to catch other people's errors. I always find that when reading another writer's manuscripts their spelling and usage errors always seem to leap off the page at me but many of my own errors remain invisible to me no matter how many times I proof read it.

I suspect that this is because the human brain is designed to recognize patterns and automatically fill in the gaps. It is this feature of the human brain that causes an author to fail to notice his own errors. His brain shows him his manuscript the way it should look instead of the way it does look.

A friend of mine from work did offer to edit my manuscripts for me. I even provided him with a copy of the manuscript of the first book I ever published, *The Theology of a Heretic*. Unfortunately, at the time I was rather anxious to publish the manuscript and my friend took too long to edit the piece. In the end I decided to dispense with his services and performed the editing myself. Kind of a shame really, as I really hate performing my own editing.

This aversion to editing applies to this very manuscript as much as it applies to all of its predecessors. By the time I have completed this particular entry the manuscript has reached the point where it is composed of 65 entries written on 106 pages. The word count has now reached nearly 32,000 words. I should edit the entries as I complete them but I am following my usual practice of procrastinating when it comes to editing. I know that I will certainly regret this later. Especially when I have a hundred entries and find myself needing to edit all of them at once. Yep, I think I'll start editing this manuscript, first thing tomorrow morning.

True to form I waited until after I had written all 100 topics before I began the editing process and I am finding the experience every bit as tedious as I expected. I was enthusiastic when I wrote Topic 13, Love and Romance. In fact, when I first conceived of this project that was one of the first topics that sprang into my mind. I greatly looked forward to writing it and when I did I felt a great deal of enthusiasm. That was one of the reasons why it is so long. I also wrote it rather quickly. I felt so inspired as I was writing it.

Then it came time to start editing it. I expected the editing to go as quickly as the writing but that did not happen. On the contrary, when I started editing the piece it took so long that I quickly grew bored with it. I found the editing so tedious that I really had to force myself to complete it. This came as quite a surprise considering my enthusiasm for the subject matter. My lack of enthusiasm for editing the piece was in stark contrast to my enthusiasm for writing it. I have found this often to be the case, at least with my own writing.

I dealt with this problem by editing one of the longer pieces then shifting my focus to the shorter pieces. I found this an effective means of dealing with my aversion to editing. It is much easier to edit a short piece than it is to edit a long piece because the tedium caused by editing does not build up as quickly when tackling the shorter pieces.

I have noticed that some professional writers speak with pride when they talk about how much material the excise from their manuscripts when they edit them. I generally don't do this. In fact, when I edit a manuscript I usually add more material to it. This is because I often get additional ideas when I am editing and I incorporate these new ideas into the manuscript. While editing *Thoughts Out of Season* I have added a couple thousand words to the original manuscript. Another reason why I add to the manuscript is that I often find that I did not adequately explain what I meant when I originally wrote my thoughts. Sometimes I am just in too much of a hurry to record my thoughts to adequately express them. Obviously, this is a deficiency that I need to correct before publishing a manuscript. Isn't that what editing is supposed to be all about?

One advantage of self-publishing over being published by the literary establishment is that I can publish whatever I want. I don't need to fulfill the marketing expectations of some corporate shill. I don't need to subject my manuscripts to some procrustean process designed to produce marketable books. Artistic self-fulfillment is the only criterion I need to meet.

15) Political Incontinence

Much as I hate spreading what is little more than a glorified rumor, I also have to admit that I find the allegation that Donald Trump paid Russian prostitutes to urinate on a bed once occupied by President Obama and his wife highly believable. It seems just like the kind of petty, juvenile prank that a man like Donald Trump would commit.

Everything that Donald Trump has said or done since winning the presidency last November has reinforced in my mind the idea that he is without a doubt the most immature and self-absorbed man ever to be elected President. He is the perfect embodiment of why the founding fathers did not want a popular vote to determine the President.

Time will only tell whether the allegations are true or not. But I suspect that they are more likely to be true than false. If the allegations are false then they were invented by someone with a deep understanding of Donald Trump's psyche.

Also, there is the strangeness in the nature of the allegations. Of all the things which a man could pay a prostitute to do, why pay her to pee on a bed? For that matter, if one were to invent allegations out of whole cloth why invent this particular allegation? It doesn't strike me as the kind of thing someone is likely to invent.

16) Henry VIII

It is well known that Henry VIII was responsible for the secession of the Church of England from the Catholic Church in 1534. It is also well known that this separation was largely caused by the refusal of the Pope to annul Henry's marriage to Catherine of Aragon despite the fact that the marriage was in direct violation of ecclesiastical law. What is not widely appreciated today was the precise nature of this separation.

Many mistakenly believe that Henry was a protestant. This was simply not the case. Henry was a staunch Catholic. He even authored a book defending Catholicism against Protestantism for which the Pope had given him the title of Defender of the Faith. Henry was no Protestant. What caused him to break the Church of England away from the Catholic Church wasn't conversion to the Protestant cause. On the contrary, it was his fervent belief in Catholicism coupled with his conviction that the papacy was fundamentally corrupt that caused him to remove the Church of England from under papal control.

Before marrying Henry, Catherine had been the wife of Henry's older brother, Arthur. As the widow of his brother, Catherine was forbidden to marry Henry under both ecclesiastical and civil law. However, Henry VII insisted upon the marriage as the consummation of a political alliance with Spain and the Hapsburg Dynasty. Henry was opposed to the marriage on legal grounds. His father reminded Henry that as a prince he was not subject to the civil law and Henry VII was able to obtain a dispensation from the Pope to allow the marriage to go forward. Catherine swore that she had never slept with Arthur, thus claiming that since the marriage was never consummated it did not legally matter.

Despite twenty four years of marriage and repeated pregnancies, Catherine of Aragon failed to produce a single viable male heir. Her only surviving child was Princess Mary. She did not help her cause by fasting during her pregnancies. By 1533 Catherine at 47 was clearly too old to produce the needed heir. Henry came to regard Catherine's failure as proof of divine disfavor. He needed to marry again for the good of the kingdom but he was too staunch a Catholic to divorce her. Instead, he petitioned the Pope for an annulment.

The annulment was denied and Henry realized that the reason that the Pope had failed to annul his illegal marriage was due to power politics rather than religious belief. Catherine was the daughter of the King of Spain and a member of the powerful Hapsburg Dynasty. She was also the cousin of the Holy Roman Emperor, Charles V. The annulment was denied because the Hapsburgs had far more influence with the Pope than Henry possessed.

By pulling the Church of England away from the Catholic Church and making himself the head of that church, Henry granted himself the authority to annul his own marriage. An annulment which he regarded as consistent with church law and God's will. Thus Henry's ecclesiastical secession did not occur because Henry had espoused Protestantism, but rather because he regarded himself as more Catholic than the Pope.

By 1533 Henry came to regard the Catholic Church as hopelessly corrupt and in desperate need of reform. In that regard he did agree with the Protestants. But unlike the Protestants, he did not regard the problems of the church as stemming from its theology but simply from the corrupting influence of its wealth.

Since Henry lacked the authority and influence to bring about that reform within the entire church, he decided to break the Church of England away from Papal authority. Once this was done he had all the authority and influence he needed to rework the church to his own liking.

While some of Henry's reforms certainly did take the Church of England into the direction of Protestantism, Henry was never a Protestant and more than a few Lutheran missionaries paid for their lives by mistaking his reforms for Protestant leanings.

How then did England become a Protestant country? Henry eventually did obtain the male heir he so desperately wanted, by his third wife, Jane Seymour. Henry then did a rather curious thing. He allowed his son and heir, Prince Edward, to be tutored by Protestants. Naturally, this caused the prince to become a protestant himself and when he succeeded his father as King Edward VI in 1547 he officially proclaimed himself a Protestant and converted the entire country.

Edward died without an heir in 1553, so the throne passed on to Mary I after a few days during which it was occupied by Lady Jane Grey. Mary was a staunch Catholic who married King Philip II, the King of Spain, and brought the Church of England back under papal authority. When Mary in turn died in 1558, the throne passed to Elizabeth I, a protestant, who again broke the Church of England away from the Catholic Church and returned it to the Protestant fold.

17) Death

When I was young I always took longevity for granted. This was a bit of foolishness shared by most youths but I had at least some rational reason to look forward to a longer than average lifespan. I had a number of recent ancestors who had lived to a ripe old age.

My great grandmother had lived ninety eight years and so had her mother. When my grandfather died at age seventy-eight his funeral was attended by all of his siblings, including his older brother.

So it came as quite a shock to me to find that I had a cancer tumor in my tongue at the age of forty-six. What made this particularly difficult to accept was the fact that I did not fit the usual profile for an oropharangeal cancer sufferer. The typical victim for that particular form of cancer was somebody like Michael Douglas, a person in their mid to late sixties who had spent their life smoking and drinking heavily.

I have never smoked or used tobacco in any other form. I was never a heavy drinker and by the time the cancer was diagnosed I had not drank a drop of alcohol for nearly twenty years. I didn't even have human papillomavirus.

My cancer was treated successfully. At the time of this writing I have been cancer free for almost five years, the clinical definition of cured. Nevertheless, I've had my complacency shattered, never to return. I no longer take longevity for granted.

At 51 I know that I am now much closer to the end of my life than I am to its beginning. Yet this knowledge does not disturb me. I don't fear death. On the contrary, there are times when I actually look forward to it. I wonder what will happen after I die but such ruminations are never accompanied by a sense of foreboding. Most of the time I contemplate my own death with a sense of detached equanimity. I like to think of death as a new beginning rather than an end. I hope that I meet my demise with a sense of adventure. The only thing I know with absolute certainty is that one day in the future I will die. I feel that it is the height of irrationality to fear that inevitability.

I have no idea how much longer I have left on this Earth, but I am resolved to make the most out of however much time I have left. A big part of that resolution involves continuing with my writing.

18) Writing

Sometimes writing comes so easily to me. Whenever I feel inspired the words just flow out of me almost effortlessly. At those times I can spend hours at a time writing and my productivity can be truly prodigious. I have written entire chapters of novels in a single sitting. When the muse really had a hold over me I had spent as much as sixteen hours writing.

I always write whenever I feel inspired. I want to take advantage of the opportunity whenever it presents itself. Such moments are magical and impossible to predict. They can happen at any time and last any length of time. The inspiration might continue for an hour or two or for an entire day. But sometimes it only lasts a few minutes.

Writing under inspiration is an incredible feeling. It is as if the words are coming from somewhere else, like I am channeling some other entity. From this experience I can see why ancient writers often claimed that their writing was inspired by gods. But I suspect that what is really happening is some sort of chemical cascade in the brain. Creativity feeding off of itself to inspire more creativity.

Then there are times when the inspiration just isn't there. Then the words come out slowly and I have to struggle for each sentence. On those days I might be lucky to write a complete paragraph.

My response to the lack of inspiration depends on how I am feeling and how determined I am to write. When I am not particularly determined and I don't really feel like writing I simply stop writing and do something else. That can be a very effective strategy. After all, I might find inspiration in the very activity I decided to substitute for writing. Some ideas for novels I have developed were inspired by movies I had watched.

When I am determined to write and I feel like writing, I will gut through it and continue to write without the inspiration. This sometimes works too. There were times when all it took to find inspiration was to re-read what I had written before. There are times when inspiration simply never comes. I just plod along unproductively. Still, some productivity is better than none at all. Sometimes I'll develop further ideas simply by thinking about a subject long enough.

Some days I just don't feel like writing at all. On those days I simply don't write more than just a sentence or two. I believe that I should always write something, even just a few words. But I also don't believe in forcing it. I have found that trying too hard to write produced results that weren't really worth the effort.

19) Late Night Thoughts

Perhaps I should call them "early morning thoughts?" Either title would have been appropriate. Traditionally, the day began with dawn. Under that scheme 3:00 a.m. would have been regarded as late night and I normally think of that time as late night. However, for the last one hundred and fifty years or so we have grown accustomed to regarding one minute after Midnight as the official beginning of the day. So, it would be no surprise if most people didn't regard 3 a.m. as early morning.

Anyway, last night I had gone to bed shortly after Midnight. Between 3 a.m. and 4 a.m. I found myself awake again and my brain working overtime. All kinds of thoughts ran through my mind. While I was experiencing this brainstorm I did not feel tired. On the contrary, I was quite alert. I only hoped that I could remember my thoughts long enough to get them down onto paper.

20) Martin Luther King, Jr.'s Birthday

By historical accident the observance of Martin Luther King, Jr.'s birthday is just four days before the inauguration day of the President of the United States. Eight years ago the first African American President took the oath of office. At the time the proximity of the inauguration with the King holiday seemed appropriately symbolic. While the inauguration of Barack Obama could hardly be described as the fulfillment of Dr. King's cherished dream of racial equality, it undeniably marked an important milestone in the journey towards the fulfillment of that dream. It was one of those rare events of such historical importance that even at the time that historical importance was readily apparent. The historical significance of most events usually does not become fully apparent until years later.

This year we see inaugurated a reactionary with an almost pathological need to obliterate every vestige of the presidency of his historic predecessor. Donald Trump is wasting no time in removing Barack Obama's appointments from office, repealing his legislation and countermanding his executive orders. He is even removing every trace of Barack Obama's eight year occupancy of the White House. This seems to go beyond the normal interparty rivalry that characterizes American politics. It's almost as if Donald Trump knows instinctively that his administration will be compared to the administration of his predecessor and that the comparison will most likely be unfavorable.

In January 2009 the fulfillment of Martin Luther King, Jr.'s dream seemed closer than it had ever been before. In January 2017 it seems to have receded farther away than it has in decades. I do not think that the election of Donald Trump was the cause of this change. Rather, I believe that his election was a symptom of it. Race relations in this country had been deteriorating for a couple of years leading into the last election. I wonder how much the controversies over the police shootings of young black men and the resulting protests and riots contributed to the election of Donald Trump.

21) The End of an Era

Ringling Brothers and Barnum and Bailey Circus will put on its last performances this May. This circus had been an American institution for 146 years. It was by far the most famous circus in America. As a child I had attended a performance of Ringling Brothers Circus when it performed in the Capital Center. By then of course, they were performing in indoor arenas rather than under the big top. Performing under a tent was just too dangerous for a circus of the size and complexity of the Ringling Brothers Circus.

Ringling Brothers was not the only circus I had attended as a child. I once saw the Clyde Bailey Cole Brothers Circus in the parking lot of the Frederick Shopping Center. Clyde Bailey was a much smaller circus and they did perform under the big top. In fact, they advertised themselves as the "largest circus under the big top."

Animal rights activists will doubtlessly be thrilled with the imminent demise of the largest and most famous circus in America. And I have to admit to a certain amount of ambivalence. After all, the performances of the animals in the circus can hardly be considered voluntary. At best it is coerced and at worst that coercion is accomplished through abuse or the threat of abuse. And yet, I still can't help but feel a sense of loss at the demise of the "Greatest Show on Earth."

22) Martin Luther King, Jr.'s Birthday Observed

Monday, January 16, 2017 will be the day when the Federal Government will observe Martin Luther King, Jr.'s birthday. All of the offices of the Federal Government will be closed for the occasion. All of the nation's post offices and banks will also be closed. The private sector, on the other hand, will not be observing the holiday, unless it is to offer sales which are more designed to increase the profits of the store than to honor the holiday. The vast majority of businesses will be open as usual.

Unless you work for the Federal Government or happen to work at a bank, I imagine you will be working on January 16th just like any other Monday. I know that I will be working.

Now that just begs the question, how can Martin Luther King's birthday be regarded as a genuine holiday when most people will be working that day? Isn't having off from work the hallmark of a true holiday? Isn't it the sine qua non for a day to even be a holiday? But then again, I often find myself working during holidays.

I worked last Thanksgiving Day. I worked last Memorial Day. I worked last Labor Day. I worked last Independence Day. As far as that goes, there have been many years when I worked Christmas Day.

So far as that goes, what do people usually do during their holidays off? Do they really observe the putative holiday? Sure, most people do observe Christmas and Thanksgiving and New Years Day, but do they really observe Memorial Day and Labor Day?

Some people do, but I get the impression that such people are in the decided minority these days. I mean, Memorial Day was supposed to be used to decorate the graves of fallen veterans. How many people do that now?

Some do, obviously. You do see flowers and wreaths and flags placed on the graves. But how many people are really involved?

Labor Day was supposed to be a demonstration of the importance of the labor force. It was meant to give the country a taste of what would happen if the entire labor force went on a general strike. The workers were all supposed to stay home and everyone else was supposed to see the whole country grind to a halt because of it. Now it seems like nothing more than just another excuse to barbeque, watch football and go shopping.

That seems to be the fate of most of our holidays. They start off as a day of commemoration and end up just being another day off.

23) Nearing the End

For the past year and a half I have worked at the Ozburn Hessey Logistics warehouse on Kriner Road. Well, the company was still called Ozburn Hessey Logistics when I first started working there, but near the end of 2016 it was acquired by Geodis and changed its name accordingly.

Anyway, the warehouse where I worked was employed in contract logistics. This means that we were contracted to provide warehousing and fulfillment services for a client, in this case Walmart's e-commerce division. We stored merchandize which Walmart was selling on its website and when customers ordered that merchandize we would ship the orders to the customers.

At the end of 2016 Walmart decided not to renew the contract. Instead they decided to fulfill their website orders using a different service. So for the last several weeks we have been preparing for the closing of our warehouse. We continued to fulfill customer orders until the end of last December. Starting with the new year we began shipping the remaining merchandize back to Walmart.

Now we are nearing the end. The warehouse is almost completely empty. We are now beginning to dismantle the racks and fixtures and to scrape the control lines from the warehouse floor. I'm not sure how much longer it will take before everything is done, perhaps another week or two.

I have to admit to feeling ambivalent about this. On the one hand my entire employment situation is completely up in the air. I have no idea whether or not I will even have a job after all is said and done. On the other hand, I'm in the mood for a change in my circumstances. I think that I would probably be better off with a different job.

Of course, that assumes that I would be able to find another job. At 51 I am not nearly as employable as I had been when I was younger. The last time I searched for a job I submitted thirty applications before I was able to find employment. Most companies simply are not willing to hire people my age, despite state and federal laws against age discrimination. Nevertheless, I am not afraid for my future. I just wish the situation would get resolved one way or another.

By the third week of January things had wound down at the warehouse to the point where I was only working five and a half hours a day. Obviously this did not do much to help my cash flow situation. I felt ambivalent about this development as well. While I knew that the loss of pay could pose a serious problem, I preferred to leave work early rather than hang around doing little or nothing productive. At least at home I could accomplish something useful, like write more.

As we reached the middle of January the situation finally became clear. On January 19th the last of Walmart's merchandize was loaded into the truck. That morning our supervisor finally revealed the company's plans for us. We will remain at the Kriner Road warehouse for one last week. Then we will all be transferred to another warehouse in Chambersburg to work for another client, Nutrisystem.

Nutrisystem sells pre-packaged food to customers who wish to lose weight. Our job will be to assemble cases of this pre-packaged food and ship it to Nutrisystem's customers. The way the process was explained to us, the packages are put together on assembly lines, just like in a factory.

The idea really didn't appeal to me. Instead of wandering around a one million square foot warehouse I would be forced to stand in one place and fill boxes for up to twelve hours a day. And that is just taking the mechanics of the job into consideration. The institutional culture at the Nutrisystem account sounded about as inviting as a Soviet Gulag, a Chinese Re-education Center or a Nazi work camp.

We heard all about the institutional culture at Nutrisystem because a number of people working at the Walmart account had previously worked at the Nutrisystem account. Add to this the fact that the supervisors at the Walmart account occasionally used sending people to Nutrisystem as a threat to ensure a proper level of diligence and you can imagine the effect of finally being informed of our impending fate had on our morale. It had been steadily declining even before then due to all the uncertainty, but having our worst fears realized really sank it to a new low.

I decided not to follow the others to Nutrisystem. The main reason was the work hours. When I had first taken employment at OHL I had no responsibilities and my schedule was completely open. But during the eighteen months of my employment my circumstances had changed. I now had responsibilities that greatly reduced the hours during which I was available to work.

I did not inform my employers of this. I simply resolved not the report for work at the end of January when I was scheduled to begin working at Nutrisystem. I did not appreciate the way the company handled the entire situation and this was my way of protesting.

I seriously doubt that the company cares anyway. I have the distinct impression that OHL had long used Nutrisystem as the dumping ground for employees they did not want. That was the only way I could explain why the corporate culture at Nutrisystem was so radically different from the corporate culture at the other accounts.

This notion was greatly reinforced by the fact that a select few people working at the Walmart account were transferred to other accounts just before the account closure. I believe that the people the company truly valued were the ones who received these last minute transfers, and I was not one of them.

It doesn't matter. I will find my own way. Either through my writing or by some other means. I am now beginning to search for a new job.

24) The Futility of Life

Whenever I contemplate my own mortality, I begin to wonder if there is really any point to anything that I do. The thought inevitably crosses my mind that nothing I do has any real lasting meaning.

Of course such thoughts presuppose that we only live once and then once we die everything comes to an end. While I have never been much of a fan of reincarnation, I do accept the immortality of the human soul. At least, whenever I think about mortality and life after death I believe that the life which we enjoy on this earth is not the sum total of our existence.

From that perspective it becomes clear that life is not lived in vain. I believe that we continue onward after death and this is one of the main reasons why I have no fear of death.

Could this just be vanity? Certainly. But it just seems like a colossal waste for us to live such short lives just to die and become worm food. What is the point of intelligence if we do not in fact possess an immortal soul? From a strictly biological perspective intelligence is completely unnecessary. Human perspicacity is far greater than that necessary to ensure survival. There has to be more to it than that. Our intelligence has to be more than the mere product of neurochemistry. It has to be more than a function of biology. After all, we share that same neurochemistry and much of that same cerebral architecture with the so-called lower animals. What is the point of our personalities if they exist for only seventy-five to hundred years and then dissipate with the cessation of brainwave functions?

The only way to learn this most fundamental of all truths is to die. What a shame it would be if we cannot profit from the obtaining of that truth. Maybe I am just a vain fool, but I cannot accept that we live once, we die once, and that is all there is to it.

25) Unsolicited Tax Advice

Today I received a letter from the Internal Revenue Service providing me with free but unsolicited tax advice. The letter informed me that I had until the end of January to sign up for health insurance through the Health Insurance Marketplace in order to avoid paying the penalty for being uninsured during 2017.

The reason I was sent this letter was because I had paid a penalty for not being insured for all of 2015. Why the IRS would assume that I was still uninsured more than a year later was unclear. If the IRS had really examined my 2015 tax return carefully, they would have noticed that I was insured for the last four months of that year.

But even if I was uninsured at the time they sent the letter, the advice they gave me was still of questionable value. After all, the Republicans in the Senate have already begun the process to repeal the Affordable Care Act along with its individual mandate. By the time I will need to file my 2017 income tax return there will be a very high probability that Congress will already have repealed it, thus rendering the IRS's warning irrelevant.

26) Inauguration Day

I did not watch the inauguration coverage on television. In fact, I have done as much as humanly possible to ignore the whole event. I do not like the fact that Donald Trump managed to get himself elected, but I am not among those who question his legitimacy. I do not respect him and have no intention of supporting him in any way. I am simply resigned to the fact that he is now the President of the United States. Now it will be interesting to see just how long he manages to stay in office.

I have noticed a certain amount of gloating from people who support Donald Trump coupled with an equal amount of disrespect for the outgoing President. Neither surprises me. In fact, it doesn't bother me and I do not feel the need to respond, except within these pages. It will be interesting how many of those people will still be gloating four years from now.

I feel that people have the right to their own opinions no matter how ill-informed. I also believe that people have a right to express those opinions. In doing so they reveal parts of themselves. I don't choose to respond to opinions with which I disagree but I might choose to limit my social interaction with people whose opinions I find too repugnant or who choose to express those opinions in ways that make them seem ignorant.

People have taken to the streets in Washington D.C. protesting Trump's inauguration. Sadly, those protests have turned violent. This doesn't surprise me, either. Nowadays protests seem to attract thugs like an open flame attracts moths. The criminal element always tries to take advantage of situations like this. After all, there is no better cover for criminal activity than a violent mass protest. The police would be far too preoccupied with containing the riot to bother with normal law enforcement. This phenomenon is not restricted to the United States. The same thing has happened during European protests.

I remember seeing news footage of a riot in Italy during which one of the rioters was killed by the Carabinieri. I remember some liberals complaining about the Carabinieri jeep running over the thug right after they had shot him. But from the footage I had seen it was clear that the Carabinieri were simply protecting themselves.

The Europeans sometimes take their protests far beyond simple rioting and turn them into full blown revolutions. This happened in Russia in 1917 and again in the Ukraine in 2014. The possibility for a protest to turn into a riot and then into a revolution has long been used by authoritarian regimes as the excuse for suppressing mass protests.

Even Britain, a country which has long prided itself on the degree of personal liberty afforded to its citizens, had a law designed to allow the authorities to disperse through the threat of violence unwanted mass protests, the infamous Riot Act. The law required the provisions of the act to be read out loud just before the forcible dispersion of the protestors. As the "Reading of the Riot Act" was sometimes followed by lethal military force being used against the protestors, the practice became synonymous with issuing an ultimatum.

Buzzfeed is actually counting down the time left in the Trump Administration down to the second. Naturally, this timer assumes that Trump will not be re-elected in 2020. Then again, given Trump's age, it is far from certain that he will even survive his term of office. Men in their 70's can appear to still be in the pink of health and then die rather unexpectedly.

27) Slasher Horror

I have long suspected that the secret to the success of slasher horror movies stemmed from the fact that most of the victims in these movies were archetypes of the elite of high school society; jocks, cheerleaders and other members of the popular cliques. These were the very types of people who made life so difficult for the lesser mortals that made up the rank and file of typical high school student bodies. The fact that these movies were often just as popular among the very people portrayed as the victims came as no real surprise. After all, no one ever accused jocks and cheerleaders of perspicacity.

But audiences of slasher horror were not limited to high school students. Adults often appreciated these movies as well and for similar reasons. The victims of slasher horror were often portrayed as engaging in the types of behavior which adults found irritating. They abuse alcohol and drugs and they indulge in sexual promiscuity. Often they are engaged in this activity just before their death scenes, making their murder almost a form of divine retribution for their irresponsible behavior.

The victims in slasher flicks also often evidence the arrogance and disrespect long associated with teenagers.

Thus their deaths can be seen as just retribution for their hubris.

Thus the slasher flick represented our own dark fantasies and as such provided us with a type of catharsis. Even if that catharsis was, by necessity, displaced. The only real danger in this was the fact that too many deluded people have trouble distinguishing between healthy fantasy and reality. Finding the ersatz catharsis offered by slasher horror ultimately unfulfilling, they used slasher horror as inspiration for achieving real catharsis in the real world.

28) Inverse Utility

In economics utility is the notion of usefulness. The more useful something is the greater its utility is said to be. I have noticed that the more useful something is to us, the more indispensible something it, the less we are willing to pay for it. I call this the Law of Inverse Utility.

To illustrate the point, I have only to remind the reader that the most important thing to them is air. We can only survive for three minutes without air, so it has to be the commodity with the greatest utility. Yet how much are you willing to pay for air? I suspect that the vast majority of people would be quite indignant at the mere suggestion that they should pay for the air that they breathe.

Water is the next most important commodity as we can only survive for three days without it. Unlike air, we are willing to pay for water, but not very much. I could make a list of commodities from the most important in terms of physical survival to the least important. The more important a commodity is, the less we are willing to pay for it.

Inverse utility works the other way as well. This is evidenced by the fact that we are often willing to spend surprisingly huge amounts of money on commodities that are completely useless. Look at how much money people are willing to pay for diamonds. Yet exactly how useful are diamonds? They have no practical use at all except as symbols of conspicuous consumption.

This works for all other commodities as well. Consider how much some people are willing to pay to own famous works of art, millions of dollars, in fact. Yet how much use do they really get out of the paintings? Seems to me that an inexpensive print could serve the same purpose, assuming that the purpose is to beautify a wall. Naturally, buying a print would miss the entire point of owning such a piece of art. Like diamonds, famous works of art are another example of conspicuous consumption. People buy them simply to prove they command the wealth to buy such items. Nothing illustrates wealth better than spending millions of dollars on something that is utterly useless. The utility in the artwork exists solely in the pride and prestige of ownership.

The Law of Inverse Utility applies to earned income as well. That is why the people who make the most useful contributions to society such as farmers and fishermen receive the lowest incomes while those who are paid the most are those who make the least important contributions, such as professional athletes and entertainers.

29) The Presidential Swing Set

My ex-wife's daughter attended the Montessori Academy in Chambersburg. On Inauguration Day she received a four page reader detailing Donald Trump's inauguration. The reader gave basic information about the duties of the President of the United States and was appropriately neutral in its treatment. On the last page was a drawing of the White House with important features prominently labeled.

Naturally, this labeling was done from a child's perspective of what was interesting and important. So, it did not surprise me that the Presidential swing set was one of the features of the White House grounds to receive this treatment.

Unfortunately, that swing set was no longer on the White House grounds. Donald Trump had the swing set removed because it had been installed by Barack Obama. Obviously, whoever prepared the reader was unaware of this fact despite the fact that it had been prominently reported by the mainstream media.

30) Inaugural Stupidity

Just to prove that the Republicans don't have a monopoly on stupidity, a group of anti-Trump protestors thought it was a good idea to throw water on attendees entering one of the inaugural events.

Exactly what this was supposed to accomplish I really don't know. It's not like they were actually throwing enough water to be more than mildly annoying. Seems to me that the only thing they really accomplished was displaying how idiotic they were.

I have always respected the right of people to protest and to voice their opinions. However, I draw the line when it comes to throwing things at people, no matter how harmless the thrown substance may be. The line between throwing water on someone, especially in the winter, and outright assaulting them is a very thin one indeed.

31) Trump's Inaugural Address

I did not watched any part of Donald Trump's inauguration. I just didn't care about it. Nevertheless, curiosity got the better of me and I ended up reading Trump's inaugural address.

I was prompted to do so after reading that George Will considered Trump's inauguration speech "the most dreadful" one ever delivered. So I performed a Google Search. I had no doubt that the full text of the speech would be on the internet somewhere. I found it on CNN's website. That's right, CNN, according to Trump the home of "fake news".

Trump's inaugural address was rather long on rhetorical blather and rather short on concrete proposals. His stated goal was undeniably ambitious. He was going to cure all of America's socio-economic ills. The achievement of such an ambitious agenda will certainly require equally ambitious policies. But the only policy which Trump's speech proposed was the rebuilding of the American economy through the implementation of protectionism.

Yes, that's right, protectionism rears its ugly head once again. I am truly astonished that a man who earned an economics degree from a prestigious business school would seriously propose protectionism as the cure for America's economic ills.

Protectionism can be carried out in two ways. The first way is to impose tariffs on imported goods in order to raise the price of those goods above the prices at which comparable domestic goods are offered. The second way is for the government to subsidize domestic goods so that they can be sold below the cost of imported goods. Naturally, the government can use both methods simultaneously.

While tariffs certainly do encourage domestic manufacturing, they do so at the expense of the consumer who must pay higher prices to obtain the goods they want. Subsidies can allow prices to remain low but the government must finance those subsidies either through increased taxation or increased debt. Either way, there will be a price for such a subsidy scheme.

The biggest problem with any protectionist scheme and the reason why they all ultimately fail is because other nations will not sit idly by while America indulges in protectionist practices. Retaliatory tariffs will be enacted by the nations directly harmed by our protectionism. Ultimately this will raise the prices not only of imported goods for which there are comparable American goods available but also for imported goods which cannot be produced domestically. Think about that next time you buy coffee, tea or cocoa.

Furthermore, I'm not at all sure that this policy would work, even if implemented. Seems to me that protectionist policies would come far too late to reverse the outsourcing of manufacturing that has been occurring for the last thirty years. Seems to me that this is an example of closing the barn door long after the horse has already run away.

But that is really only relevant if Trump's speech represents a serious policy proposal and not merely a rhetorical bone thrown to the American public. It is also only relevant if the Republicans in Congress actually go along with it. Somehow I find it very hard to believe that the plutocrats who now run the Republican Party will really allow such an agenda to be carried out. After all, how could Walmart continue to offer low prices if they had to sell goods made in America instead of China?

I noticed the conspicuous absence of any references to his proposed wall along the Mexican border. Does this mean he's given up on the idea or simply decided not to mention it? If he imagines that such a wall would really stop illegal immigration then he is seriously deluded. The illegal immigrants will still come in. They'll just have to sail around the wall, fly over it or tunnel under it. Where there is a will there is always a way.

The most bizarre part about Trump's speech was his claim that his inauguration represented the people taking back their government. This is a very strange claim for a man who did not garner the majority of the popular vote. Trump owed his electoral victory to the quirks of the electoral college and not due to any popular mandate to lead the country. Even in the electoral college his victory was less than impressive. Had he not won the state of Pennsylvania and one or two other states, he would not have won the election at all. Neither he nor Hilary Clinton would have had enough electoral votes to win outright which would have caused the election to be decided by the House of Representatives. Given Trump's lack of political support in the House of Representatives before his election, you can imagine how the House would have voted.

32) Swallowing

Most people don't realize how complex the act of swallowing really is. As long as everything works well they do not appreciate how many muscles and organs are involved in swallowing their food.

While people fully appreciate the role their teeth play in eating by cutting and grinding their food in preparation for swallowing, they usually do not appreciate the critical role played by the tongue. The tongue moves the food around the mouth so that the various types of teeth can be brought to bear on the food. The tongue also moves the masticated food into the back of mouth and down into the throat. While it is certainly much more difficult to eat without teeth, it is still possible. Without a tongue, however, eating and swallowing are not possible at all.

The throat is composed of two structures, the pharynx and the larynx. Food must pass through both the pharynx and the larynx in order to travel from the mouth to the esophagus.

At the beginning of the swallowing process the soft palate tenses and is pulled up to close off the nasopharanx so that the food cannot enter the nose. Muscles of the throat pull the oropharynx forward and upwards to facilitate the entry of the food into the pharynx. After the food enters the pharynx the tongue closes off the pharynx to prevent the food from returning to the mouth. Peristalsis of the muscles of the pharynx then drives the food downward into the larynx.

The vocal cords close over the trachea, sealing it off to prevent food from becoming aspirated. The hyoid bone is raised which pushes the pharynx and larynx up higher. Breathing is interrupted while the food passes through the throat. This condition is known as deglutition apnea.

Once the food has entered the esophagus the muscles of the throat relax causing the larynx and pharynx to return to their original positions. Esophageal peristalsis carries the food down into the stomach.

In 2012 I had part of my tongue surgically removed and replaced with a piece of my thigh muscle. While I am capable of swallowing my tongue has become tethered to the floor of my mouth. Therefore, it lacks the mobility necessary to assist in chewing my food or to move the food into my throat. Because of this I now have dysphagia, an inability to eat solid food. I can swallow liquids but I cannot swallow anything thicker than the consistency of applesauce.

33) Money

Trade has existed since before the recording of history. In fact, it is quite likely that trade at some level has existed for as long as there have been human beings.

The earliest form of trade was barter and for uncounted millennia it was probably the only form of trade possible. By far the biggest drawback to barter was the fact that for a barter exchange to occur each party to the exchange had to possess something the other party wished to have. If I hate mushrooms I am not likely to want to trade my berries to you in exchange for your mushrooms, no matter how favorable the terms might be.

The answer to the barter problem was to find something with such universal appeal than no one would refuse to trade for it. If everyone wanted it then it could be exchanged for anything else. Such items would become accepted by custom as mediums of exchange, money.

Theoretically anything could be money, seashells, pieces of amber, bits of volcanic glass, colored rocks. The only requirement was that custom had to place an intrinsic value upon a commodity that was universally accepted.

Whatever commodity custom established as the medium of exchange would quickly become the standard of wealth. Custom would eventually determine the relative value of all goods and services when compared to the medium of exchange. If custom allowed blue seashells to become the medium of exchange then custom would soon also determine how many blue seashells one needed to buy a pound of flour or an ounce of butter. Everything would be valued in terms of blue seashells and eventually all wealth would be counted in terms of blue seashells. Determining an individual's wealth would be a matter of inventorying all of his belongings and then calculated how many blue seashells would be required to purchase all of them.

Now we know that the earliest standards of wealth were livestock, orchards and cultivated acreage. This is why I suspect that the earliest form of money was some form of agricultural product, most likely flour. Everybody needs food and while not everyone likes mushrooms or berries I can't imagine anyone not liking flour.

Flour seems to fulfill all of the requirements for a medium of exchange. It is universally demanded and it has intrinsic value. It is also portable. However, flour does have certain disadvantages as a medium of exchange.

While it does have intrinsic value, that value is quite low. So, a great deal of flour would be needed in order to purchase other commodities. Flour has a limited shelf life. It grows stale and it molders. This also reduces its value as a medium of exchange and a standard of wealth.

The best medium of exchange was a commodity that did not spoil or decay, one that was portable, one that could not be manufactured, one that was sufficiently rare to have a high intrinsic value and one that was universally demanded. The two commodities that best fulfilled all of these conditions were silver and gold.

So, it was only natural that silver and gold should become the mediums of exchange early in the history of western civilization. Once established as the twin mediums of exchange, silver and gold became the standards of wealth. Wealth then became measured in terms of weights of silver and gold such as the talent or the pound.

No doubt wealthy merchants began paying a share of their profits to the government in order to obtain their protection. Traveling the trade routes was dangerous in ancient times. Bandits often prowled the roads, especially in the wilderness between cities or near the borders of kingdoms. This was most likely the origin of taxation. Once governments began taxing mercantile activity they gained a vested interest in that activity. Governments then saw obvious advantages in promoting mercantilism.

Governments saw the need to secure their borders, build roads between their cities and keep those roads free of bandits. Governments also took steps to assure that the merchants weren't cheated or that the governments themselves were not cheated. Thus the governments standardized the weights and measures used in commercial transactions. Naturally, this would include the weights used in weighing silver and gold in determining payments.

Once silver and gold had become accepted as the standard of wealth, it became necessary to keep track of exactly how much silver and gold was present. This would be exceedingly difficult unless the silver and gold were stored in a way that made inventorying it more convenient. The most obvious way to do this was to cast weights of silver and gold of uniform size, weight and purity.

Thus silver and gold intended for use as money was cast into bars or plates. Of course, silver and gold were both also utilized in all types of items, many of them for everyday use. However, whenever the need for more money arose, these items were always melted down and the silver and gold cast into bars or plates.

I suspect that the adoption of silver and gold as mediums of exchange increased the demand for silver and gold objects. The use of silver and gold in objects, especially objects for everyday use, became a form of conspicuous consumption. What better way for a man to display his wealth than to use a portion of it to provide himself with ordinary housewares. Why drink from a wooden cup when one could drink from a golden one? Why wear clothing made from wool or linen when one could wear cloth made from silver or gold thread?

The first coins were minted in Lydia in the 6th century B.C. They were quickly accepted as the medium of exchange throughout the Mediterranean world and emulated by everyone else. Coins were standardized in both weight and purity which made them superior to the crude weights used for money before their invention. The fact that coins could be issued in various denominations made them eminently versatile. So successful were coins in winning acceptance as money that they came to be regarded as the only thing accepted as such, then they became synonymous with money.

We often entertain the rather strange notion that governments are somehow fundamentally different from us. We use the very term 'government' as if it were somehow something alien. But the fact is that government is really nothing more than an institution made up of people. Because of that the motivations of government are the motivations of the people who make up the government, especially the leaders of the government. There is no fundamental difference between government officials and ourselves. They are part of the very same culture as we are. Because of this governments share many of the same motivations as individuals.

Just as individuals seek to increase their income and their wealth, so does government. In the past governments had four ways of increasing their wealth. The first way was to increase taxes. This was the simplest and easiest method but it often led to popular resentment, sometimes even driving the people into open rebellion.

Hammurabi once sent a letter admonishing one of his provincial governors for taxing the people too excessively. The king advised the governor that he must "shear the sheep, not flay them." Hammurabi hit upon a fundamental truth. If government taxes too heavily, it runs the risk not only of inciting rebellion but of undermining the economy, thus reducing future tax revenue.

The second way was to promote economic development and thereby increase the tax base. This was done whenever possible and in fact was a method which has been employed since the beginning of recorded history. This was the reason for ancient irrigation projects and colonization, the draining of swamps and the clearing of forests. This is why western Europeans began systematically exploring the world in the middle of the 15th century.

The third way was to plunder the wealth of their neighbors. This method was employed a great deal more at the beginning of antiquity but it has been indulged in as recently as the middle of the twentieth century. Some of the more cynical claim that it is still being employed today, but if so nobody is willing to admit to it. Of course, this method can only be employed if one has neighbors worth plundering who are not also too powerful to conquer.

The fourth way was to debase the coinage by reducing the purity of the gold and silver in the coins so that the government could mint more of them. This method was employed by the Roman Empire because they found that the other three methods were no longer available to them.

The ancient Romans made a mistake commonly made by government officials. They grow so arrogant that they believe that they can impose their will upon the people by legislative fiat. They forgot that it was custom which determined what was money and how much it was worth rather than government regulation.

When the Romans debased their coinage they undermined public confidence in their currency. The result was a devaluation of the coinage. Custom accepted only silver and gold as money. The Roman currency was accepted as money because it was made of unadulterated silver and gold. When that proved to no longer be the case, the value of the currency as money became proportional to the amount of actual silver and gold in the coins. Yes, the Roman government could steadily mint more and more coins but as it did so the value of those coins steadily declined.

The development of banking which began in the 14th century ushered in a financial revolution that created both new ways of creating income and new forms of money. By far the most important innovation introduced by banking was compound interest.

With the use of compound interest wealth could be created for the first time since agricultural products had been replaced by silver and gold as the standards of wealth. Banks paid compound interest to depositors in order to encourage them to save their money. The banks then lent those deposits to borrows at higher rates of compound interest, thus ensuring that the banks themselves profited. In both the paying of interest and the lending of money banks became the new creators of money. With the rise of banking, currency ceased to be the only form of money and governments lost their monopoly on the creation of money.

A bank creates new wealth every time it lends money to a borrower. This is true regardless of the purpose of the loan. This happens every time a bank lends money to the government, every time a bank lends money to a business or non-profit organization to finance construction or business expansion, every time a bank lends money to an individual for a home loan, a home equity loan, a car loan, a student loan or a business loan.

Banks also create new money by developing financial instruments which gain universal acceptance as mediums of exchange. The first such documents were Letters of Credit.

Banks began as institutions designed to promote trade by lending investment capital to merchants. The first banks were established in major mercantile cities, beginning in Italy in the 14th century. The largest banking houses established branch offices in many cities so that they could better serve their mercantile clients.

In an age where money only existed in the form of gold and silver coins, transporting large amounts of cash was both inconvenient and highly risky. The banks solved this problem by issuing Letters of Credit.

A merchant would deposit money into a bank and the bank would issue a Letter of Credit certifying that the cash was on deposit. The holder of the Letter of Credit could redeem the Letter for the deposited money, either at the bank which originally issued the Letter or one of its branch offices.

As the Letter of Credit was backed by the deposit of gold and silver coins, it was held to have a monetary value equal to the backing deposit. Merchants and banks came to accept Letters of Credit as a new form of money. They could be used to make purchases and settle debts, at least within the banking and mercantile circles.

Obviously, Letters of Credit were very limited in either circulation or utility, mainly because of the large amounts of money involved. Because of these limitations, they were not able to seriously challenge gold and silver coins as commonly used mediums of exchange. Banks needed a new financial instrument which would not suffer from these limitations and therefore could potentially displace gold and silver coins as mediums of exchange. The banks developed just such a financial document when they invented the bank note.

Banks notes are paper currency issued by a bank. Like Letters of Credit, bank notes originally derived their value from the fact that the notes were backed by gold and silver coins held on deposit by the bank. As the bank notes were issued in various denominations which were small enough for use in everyday transactions, they quickly became popular. One did not have to be a banker or wealthy merchant to find the bank note useful.

Once bank notes won general acceptance as a form of money, governments quickly saw the advantage of converting the private notes into legal tender. After all, it was much cheaper to print a bank note than it was to mint a coin. Furthermore, bank notes gave governments a way of issuing money without having to deplete their gold reserves. While the early bank notes could be exchanged at will for their value in silver or gold, few people bothered to do so. After all, the bank notes themselves were accepted everywhere.

Look at the currency in your own wallet. A close inspection of the dollar bill reveals that it was issued by one of the regional Federal Reserve Banks. Foreign currency is issued by foreign banks. British Pound Notes are issued by the Bank of England.

Bank notes were accepted to have monetary value because they were backed by silver and gold deposited somewhere. If not in the banks themselves, then in the treasuries of the governments which were now backing those bank notes.

During the Great Depression the finance ministries of all of the important countries, the United States among them, carried out a daring experiment. They took their currencies off the silver and gold standards. This meant that the bank notes were no longer backed by silver and gold deposits and could no longer be exchanged for silver and gold.

Why was this done? Because for as long as a nation's currency was on the gold or silver standard then the value of that currency was set by statute. When the dollar was on the gold standard, the dollar was defined as being worth a fraction of an ounce of gold. This meant two things. First, that the value of the dollar could never change. Second, that the value of gold could never change. By removing the dollar from the gold standard, both the value of the dollar and the value of gold could change. In fact, the value of both now fluctuates on a hourly basis.

Of course, the governments took the enormous risk that removing the world's currencies from the gold and silver standards would cause the public to lose faith in the currency and cause it to lose its status as money. This has happened in some countries, at least temporarily. It happened to Germany in the 1920's. But it has not happened to most of the other world's currencies.

Why not? Perhaps because that by the time the currencies were removed from the gold and silver standards most of the money in the world did not take the form of gold, silver or currency. What form did most of the world's money take, then? The form of balances in bank accounts.

Obviously this was a slow process that took several centuries to occur and just as obviously, it was the banking industry rather than government finance ministries which carried out that process.

Bank accounts have existed since the invention of banking in 14th century Italy. At first they were nothing more than vehicles for recording financial transactions. This changed as bankers sought to make finance more convenient for their customers. Towards that end they invented financial instruments which eventually took the place of coins as money. In an effort to make banking ever more convenient the bankers developed financial instruments that were increasingly flexible. As the use of these financial instruments was so much more convenient than using either coins or bank notes in time the financial instruments displaced coins and bank notes as the principle forms of money. Once that happened silver and gold ceased to be the only forms of money accepted by custom. As custom determines the nature of money, once custom came to accept financial instruments in place of gold and silver it no longer became critically important for the financial instruments to be backed by gold and silver. Once that point was reached, custom would allow the ledger balances of bank accounts to replace silver and gold as money.

The innovation that began that process was the check. By allowing their customers to write checks directly against the balance of their accounts, bankers fundamentally transformed the nature of money itself. As with every other banking innovation, at first the check was only available to wealthy individuals, business concerns and government agencies.

In time the use of checking accounts spread downward through the social strata until they became almost universal. By now the execution of a personal check has become the preferred means of settling debts. I have yet to meet a landlord who wished his rent paid in cash. Every one of my landlords has wanted to be paid by check.

The use of checks to settle debts has grown so ubiquitous that the vast majority of people now receive their pay in the form of checks. Of course, there are still some people who are paid in cash but they are decidedly in the minority. And most of them are being paid on an informal basis.

With the widespread use of checks to transfer sums between bank accounts, the need for currency and coins diminished as currency and coins were no longer necessary to affect those transfers. Thus the use of checks effectively divorced money from currency and coins. So when the finance ministries in the 1930's removed the world currencies from the gold and silver standards they were merely ratifying a process that had already occurred. Money had already been effectively divorced from silver and gold even before the governments of the world had taken action.

In its own way the next banking innovation was as revolutionary as compound interest or checking. It was the bank card. The ultimate in banking convenience, the bank card allows instant access to bank accounts, twenty-four hours a day, seven days a week, in virtually every location on earth. The bank card promises to displace currency and coins even more thoroughly than the check did.

The reason that checks did not completely displace currency and coins was because they never quite won universal acceptance. Many small businesses simply will not accept checks as payment. Also, most people do not like the write checks for small amounts. They still prefer to use cash for small purchases.

Bank cards included both debit and credit cards. With a credit card, a consumer not only has complete access to his bank accounts but can even spend money which has not been earned yet. It simply doesn't get any more convenient than that.

Like checking accounts, bank cards were initially only available to the wealthy, businesses and government agencies. But as the institutions issuing credit cards proliferated, the terms under which credit cards were issued liberalized to the point where just about everyone had one. As there are now few consumers who do not have at least one bank card, there are now few businesses that will not accept them as payment.

Another feature which caused bank cards to earn greater acceptance than checks was the greater security offered by bank card transactions. One problem with checks is that it is a simple matter for a customer to write a check for more than he has in his account. A merchant who accepts a check runs the risk that the check will be dishonored by the bank. This is not a problem with a bank card because the technology for processing the transaction allows the merchant to instantly verify that there are sufficient funds or credit available for the purchase. This has made the acceptance of bank cards for payment even safer than accepting cash. After all, bank notes can be forged or altered.

In a very real sense the bank card and the bank account backing it is now the new form of money. It is possible to set up a business, accept payments from customers, pay employees and suppliers all without touching either currency or coins. Every transaction can be carried out through the use of bank cards and electronic transfers.

But the banking industry's efforts at increasing customer convenience did not end there. Bankers continue to innovate and the most recent innovations were direct deposit and direct debit. Direct debit and direct deposit are both becoming increasingly popular. Increasingly the government is using direct deposit to pay benefits rather than executing checks. More and more employers are using direct deposit to pay their employees' salaries. More and more businesses are encouraging their customers to pay their bills through some form of electronic transfer rather than mailing in checks. Electronic transfers of funds are clearly the way of the future. Even parking meters and vending machines can now accept bank cards for payment. It is becoming increasingly easy to see a future where currency and coins will be antiquated relics. The technology already exists to completely replace currency and coins with bank card transactions. The only thing holding back to complete elimination of currency and coin is public will to use the new technology and conveniences in place of old fashioned currency and coins.

34) Air China

I purchased two one way tickets from New York to Chengdu, China so that my roommate's parents could return home next month. I booked the tickets through Air China's American website and paid for them with my ATM card. Everything seemed to go well until I pushed the "purchase" button to complete the transaction. Then, instead of receiving a confirmation like I have every other time I have ever purchases airline tickets online, I received an error page telling me that there was a problem with the transaction and I should contact my financial institution.

I had already signed up for online banking so it was a simple matter to log-in to my account and verify that Air China had charged my bank account for the price of the tickets. Clearly, the transaction had gone through. I imagine that my booking was actually present in Air China's computer system, it was just a matter of finding it. However, without a confirmation number or an e-ticket number, locating the transaction might prove challenging.

I returned to the Air China website and tried to see if I could find the booking. The website had a dedicated search engine for such inquiries. Unfortunately, the search engine required the confirmation number and the e-ticket number to perform the search. Since I had neither, I was not able to use it.

Next, I logged-in to my roommate's e-mail account. I had used my roommate's e-mail when making the booking. So, if the system sent a confirmation e-mail, it would have sent it there. A quick check of the inbox revealed no e-mails from Air China.

Finally, I tried calling the 800 customer service number on the website. After waiting for fifteen minutes during which I had to press the number '1' every five minutes to stay on hold, I finally spoke with a customer service representative. I could tell from the woman's accent that she was a Chinese national. But even if that had not been a dead giveaway the fact that she had initially answered the phone in Chinese made it glaringly obvious.

Once I had established that I only spoke English we were able to proceed. The situation was not helped by the fact that ever since the partial glossectomy which I endured nearly five years ago my ability to speak has been somewhat impaired. People often have difficulty understanding what I say over the telephone. This difficulty obviously must be added to the difficulty in speaking with someone whose command of the English language is obviously less than complete.

The customer service representative initially asked for the confirmation numbers and e-ticket numbers of my recent booking. I did not have either of those because of the failure of the website to provide me with a confirmation of the booking.

When I could not provide the requested information, the customer service representative asked for the flight numbers. I did not remember the flight numbers and I did not have the foresight to record them while I had been making the booking. When I admitted to my lack of foresight, the customer service representative asked from which airport the flight would be departing.

Now we seemed to be making some headway as I was able to inform her that the first flight would originate from JFK International Airport in New York. That narrowed the possibilities to either CA 990 or CA 982. Unfortunately, I did not remember which one. I tried telling her that I flight I had booked had been scheduled to leave New York at 1:50 p.m. Unfortunately, she was not able to understand me and when her frustration grew too great she hanged up on me.

Further action had to wait until after my roommate had returned home. Unlike me, her speech was not impaired and she was a native speaker of Chinese so she would obviously have a much easier time of communicating with the Chinese customer service representatives at Air China.

At least, that was the theory. The first time she called the customer service representative who answered the phone was a man. I have no idea what exactly was said because the conversation was completely in Chinese. I only know that after a very short discussion the customer service representative suddenly terminated the call. I think my roommate was as surprised by this as I was.

Fortunately, my roommate is not someone who is easily daunted. She immediately called Air China back. My roommate's second call was far more fruitful. This time she did not have to wait fifteen minutes before her call was answered. And this time the customer service representative made more of an effort to help us.

Four hours later Air China sent my roommate an e-mail. The e-mail itself was in Chinese but attached was a copy of the itinerary for the flights I had booked earlier. The itinerary was in both Chinese and English.

Now that I had the e-ticket numbers and the confirmation numbers I was able to use the dedicated search engine on Air China's website to verify the booking.

35) Trump and Trade

President Trump just backed out of the Trans-Pacific Partnership. This was hardly a surprise as this was a trade deal negotiated by the Obama administration that had not yet been approved by the Senate. It's just another example of Trump attempting to undo everything which President Obama had accomplished during his eight years in the Oval Office. It is also an example of Trump fulfilling at least some of his campaign promises.

As Trump withdrew from the Trans-Pacific Partnership, he cited it as the type of trade deal which he found completely unacceptable. He is opposed to multinational trade agreements as a matter of principle. Trump believes that all trade agreements must only be made on an individual basis.

Trump also wants the freedom to break out of a trade agreement upon the delivery of a thirty day termination notice. That way if a nation "misbehaves" Trump would have the power to break off trade with the offender.

It will be interesting to see just what sort of behavior Trump will regard as liable to trigger such a termination. It will be equally interesting to see just how many of our trade partners will be willing to enter into such agreements. After all, if Trump can unilaterally break his trade agreements at will, they won't be of much value as agreements, will they?

It seems to me that Trump intends to manage foreign trade the same way Walmart deals with suppliers. Trump will undoubtedly try to use America's position as the number one economy in the world to wrest concessions from other countries the same way Walmart uses its position as the number one retailer in the world to force suppliers to lower their wholesale prices.

Naturally, such a strategy is far more likely to work when applied on a one on one basis. Undoubtedly, this is the source of Trump's aversion to multilateral trade agreements. This is also probably the reason why he hopes that the European Union disintegrates. With Europe politically and economically united it simply is not possible for Trump to deal with the member states on a one on one basis.

I think that it is obvious that Trump expects the rest of the world to tolerate his protectionist policies without retaliation. Doubtlessly, that was what he meant by "misbehavior". It will be very interesting to see how this all plays out over the next couple of years. I suspect that Trump will not be able to have his way in the arena of international trade and I suspect that opposition to his policies will arise from surprising sources. It will be interesting to see how the plutocrats who now control the Republican Party will react when Trump's own brand of jingoism begins to cut into their bottom lines.

36) Trump's Family

I have never understood the predilection of the mainstream press to go after the family members of the President. While the President himself certainly should be willing to bear the honor of being a target with equanimity, grace and dignity, I don't see why this has to extend to his immediate family as well.

While the public certainly has the right to know about the actions and character of the man who occupies the Oval Office, I don't believe that the public has the same right with regards to the President's family members. I don't believe that press coverage of the President's family is necessary, proper or fair. This is especially true when those family members are minors. A ten year old certainly should not have his every move analyzed by some self appointed pundit in the press just because he happens to be the son of an unpopular president.

This did not start with Trump, either. It has been going on for decades. I can still remember the unflattering portrayals in the press of Billy Carter, President Jimmy Carter's brother. No doubt *Saturday Night Live* will parody Barron Trump in the same way they parodied Amy Carter in the late '70's. And such a parody would be just as ill-aimed.

By all means heap as much ridicule and derision as you can upon the occupant of the Oval Office himself. I suspect Donald Trump will provide all the material the press and the comedians could possibly use. By all means chortle as the new chief executive demonstrates repeatedly that he possesses none of the equanimity, grace and dignity befitting his high office. But please leave the rest of his family out of it. Criticizing the President for wallowing in the muck of the gutter comes across as so much hypocrisy when those doing the criticizing have joined him there.

37) A Seriously Flawed Analogy

I have noticed the growing popularity on social media of an analogy being drawn between President Trump and an airline pilot. According to the analogy an American citizen hoping for Donald Trump to fail as President was akin to the passenger on an airliner hoping that the pilot crashes the plane. Obviously, both the original author and the posters of this analogy are Trump supporters. Also just as obvious to anyone who can think for themselves and reflects upon the analogy that it is seriously flawed. The flaw is so deep, in fact, that it is actually fatal to the analogy.

The fatal flaw in the analogy is this: while flying an airliner has a very concrete definition of success and an equally concrete definition of failure, the governing of a nation as large and as complex as the United States is not nearly this simple. If it was then anybody could do it. Then again, Trump supporters obviously believe that anyone could do it, which is why they voted for Trump in the first place.

The other aspect of the analogy which renders it fatally flawed is this: the consequences of failure to fly the airliner are catastrophic and affect all of the passengers equally. Similarly, the benefits of success accrue to all of the passengers equally. This never happens with political policies. For every policy there are those who benefit and those who are harmed. A wise policy is one which benefits the most people while harming the fewest.

So while an airline pilot who successfully flies the plane will benefit everyone and harm no one. This will not happen with political policies, no matter how well designed or how well implemented. Someone will always be harmed.

Furthermore, failure to fly the airliner successfully means only one thing, the pilot crashed the plane with a high degree of likelihood of killing everyone onboard. In contrast, the failure of a President to manage the Federal Government can mean many things. It could mean starting World War III and destroying the entire country, but this is highly unlikely. It could also mean the complete failure of the President to implement his agenda, which may or may not harm the country as a whole depending on the nature of that agenda and the challenges facing the nation at the time.

If the President's agenda included policies that were clearly detrimental to the interests of the people then the failure of the President to implement them would hardly be catastrophic. On the contrary, such an outcome could well be the avoidance of a catastrophe.

Perhaps when liberals say they want Trump to fail as President, they might not mean that they wish for him to drive the country into ruin. Perhaps they simply mean that they hope that he fails to carry out the more bone-headed policies which he suggested during the election campaign, such as building the wall along the Mexican border, the mass deportations of millions of illegal immigrants, or the banning of immigrants from countries with Muslim majorities.

Peace and prosperity are what the American public crave. If the country enjoys both during a President's term of office than he is likely to be regarded by the public as a successful president regardless of whether his policies actually contributed to that peace and prosperity. However, I do not believe that either the managerial style of Donald Trump or the policies which he wants to pursue will be conducive to promoting either peace or prosperity.

The failure of Trump's policies are not equivalent to the failure of the country and the success of those policies are not equivalent to the success of the country. Trump's policies will benefit some but harm others. It just remains to be seen how many people will be benefitted and how many will be harmed.

One example of the airliner analogy concluded with the comment that wishing Trump to fail as President was pathetic. No, what is pathetic is the overly simplistic black and white thinking that makes someone even think that the analogy was even close to appropriate. What is pathetic is the popularity of such a clearly flawed analogy and the apparent inability of some people to think for themselves. I imagine that these are the same people who let Rush Limbaugh tell them what to think about the issues.

38) Breitbart

I never visit the Breitbart website. In fact, until the last election I had never heard of the news organization. The only contact I ever have with them is the occasional Facebook post which appears on my wall because one of my Facebook friends had commented on it.

The tone of these posts is always very snide. They come across to me as both highly unprofessional and extremely biased. I would never rely on Breitbart for serious information and I don't intend to waste my time visiting their websites. And that doesn't even take into consideration accusations of the organization's breaches of journalistic ethics, their blatant exaggerations and factual inaccuracies.

Conservative commentators are fond of accusing the mainstream media of liberal bias. This doesn't seem to prevent major scandals involving liberal politicians from appearing in the newspapers or on the television news, however. The *Washington Post* not only reported on the Monica Lewinsky scandal, it also published the Starr Report in its entirety. And I have never seen the mainstream media pander to a Democratic administration the way that Breitbart appears to be pandering to the Trump Administration.

39) The UPS Store

Yesterday I took a packet of documents to the local UPS Store with the intention of sending via UPS to their destination. The documents in question were an application for a Chinese Visa for my roommate's daughter along with the necessary supporting documents. When I arrived at the UPS Store location in Chambersburg I found the place abandoned.

The next day I performed several internet searches to see if the store had moved to another location or had gone out of business altogether. After consulting both the UPS website and the website of the local store, I found that the UPS Store was an independently owned franchise. Since the website of the Chambersburg UPS Store still listed the address I had visited the day before, it must not have relocated, rather it must have gone out of business.

40) Voter Fraud

Donald Trump cannot accept that he lost the popular vote by three million votes. He is so unwilling to admit this that he is attributing his "loss" to widespread voter fraud. He is alleging that three to five million illegal immigrants voted for Hilary Clinton, thus inflating her polling numbers.

There is no evidence that such widespread voter fraud occurred. On the other hand, evidence for Donald Trump's lack of popularity can be seen on every hand. It can be seen by anyone who does not cast a blind eye to it.

Donald Trump has recently announced that he will order the Justice Department to investigate this alleged voter fraud. But it appears that this investigation will be limited to the states which Donald Trump had lost in the election. What are the odds that this will be a fair and impartial investigation?

Howard Stern made a very interesting observation on his radio show. He suggested the possibility that Trump's voter fraud investigation might have been prompted by the fact that Trump had unexpectedly won the election. Perhaps Trump never intended to win the election in the first place and is hoping for a way out. While I have to admit to finding this a highly provocative possibility, I cannot take it seriously. Mainly because of Trump's announced intention to limit the investigate to states which he lost. If he wanted to overturn his own election wouldn't he be focusing on the states which he won by a narrow margin? Also, if Trump wants out of the White House he has only to resign. He need not concoct a phony investigation as an exit strategy.

41) Urban Planning

Living in Chambersburg for the past seven years has given me quite an appreciation for good urban planning. This has been largely because good urban planning has not been among the amenities which the inhabitants of Chambersburg enjoy.

Every afternoon I am caught in traffic jams on my way home because there only appears to be one road out of town in each direction. Exacerbating this situation is the fact that there are three exits from Interstate 81 providing access to Chambersburg. The next closest exits are located miles away. This means that a lot of people who live in Franklin County must pass through Chambersburg in order to use the interstate.

Thus, a large amount of the traffic contributing to the traffic jams in downtown Chambersburg are motorists who are only passing through the town on the way to outlying communities. They neither live there, work there or shop there. And all of them are trying to use those same four roads out of town.

Most the traffic seems to use the roads leading east and west, Lincoln Way East and Lincoln Way West, respectively. Exacerbating this problem are two choke points, one on each road. The choke point on Lincoln Way East is just west of the Walker Road/Stouffer Avenue intersection. There the west bound lanes narrow from two lanes to one lane. The choke point on Lincoln Way West is located just west of Grandview Avenue. Again the road narrows from two lanes to one.

The Lincoln Way West choke point is especially annoying because the road is only one lane for only a single block before it widens again to two lanes.

Both choke points cause traffic to back up every time the volume is heavy. These backups make it difficult for cars to enter the road from side streets or parking lots. Because of the lack of adequate urban planning drivers often have no alternative routes available and therefore must use Lincoln Way East or Lincoln Way West.

Personally, I would not use Lincoln Way East or Lincoln Way West if I had any viable alternatives. But unfortunately, the apartment complex where I live only has street access to Lincoln Way West. So I have no choice but to use it.

42) Wearing Your Heart on Your Bumper

Decorating the rear bumpers of vehicles with bumper stickers has been practiced for decades. For as long as I can remember, in fact, and probably for many decades before then. In recent years the stickers have not been limited to the rear bumpers. It seems that every available space on the rear of the vehicle, including the rear window now sports one or more decorative stickers.

People often enjoy using these stickers to personalize their vehicles. In the process they often reveal quite a bit about themselves. They tell us who they vote for, what schools they attend, what kinds of pets they have, which musical artists they listen to. Some of these stickers tell the whole world the size and exact composition of the owner's family. Some of these stickers serve as memorials for recently deceased family and friends.

I never put bumper stickers or any other type of sticker on the back of my car. The reason is simple. I don't believe that it is prudent to reveal any more about myself than is absolutely necessary. Some people are just not likely to appreciate which political candidates you support or what personal philosophy you espouse. And some people are sufficiently sociopathic to demonstrate that lack of appreciation violently.

Take one case in point. A motorist driving through downtown Chicago was pulled out of his car and assaulted by a group of thugs who took violent exception to the fact that he had voted for Donald Trump. How would those thugs have known this? Did they know their victim personally? I don't think so. I believe that they pulled him out of his car and assaulted him because he had a Trump/Pence bumper sticker on the rear bumper of his car.

Is this blaming the victim? Perhaps. I am certainly not condoning the actions of the thugs and I certainly agree with the notion that we should all feel free to reveal as much about ourselves as we wish without fear of retribution. The motorist was certainly not at fault for revealing his political affiliations and the thugs were certainly not entitled to beat him for it. I think that the thugs should be prosecuted to the fullest extent of the law. Ideally such incidents should never happen, but the real world is often not in accordance with our ideals and prudence demands dealing realistically with such harsh realities.

43) Waterboarding

I was not surprised to find Donald Trump advocating the use of waterboarding. Disgusted and dismayed, yes, but not surprised. Trump seemed determined to take every opportunity to prove that he is every bit as bad a President and every bit as bad a human being as I believed he was when he was merely a candidate for the presidency.

Waterboarding was a diabolical torture method first employed by the Spanish Inquisition in the 15th century. That alone should make us extremely reluctant to use it. But Trump clearly wasn't troubled by such considerations. The only thing he seemed to care about is that it seemed to work.

But did it work? While waterboarding was certainly effective in convincing even the most recalcitrant prisoner to speak, I am not convinced that the information obtained in that way was truly accurate. The problem with waterboarding, as with every method of torture, was its very effectiveness in eliciting responses. The victim of torture will do anything to stop the torture, even lie. Torture undeniably provided information, but all too often that information was inaccurate and unreliable.

But even if waterboarding were proven to be a hundred percent effective, we have no business employing it. As Albert Camus once observed when commenting upon French use of torture during Algeria's war for independence in the 1950's "one cannot fight the good fight with evil weapons."

That is because the employment of evil weapons and evil methods of obtaining information cannot help but corrupt those who employ them and in the end undermine the very cause in which those weapons and methods were used.

While ruthlessness certainly provided its practitioners with a substantial tactical advantage, it also hampered its practitioners with strategic disadvantages that far outweigh those tactical advantages. When fighting against a ruthless opponent it was always better to maintain the moral high ground and refrain from joining in the enemy's ruthlessness. Otherwise you became just as bad as the enemy against which you were fighting. Remember Nietzsche's warning about fighting with monsters: "Whoever fights with monsters must take care he does not become a monster." By adopting the ruthlessness of our enemy for the sake of remaining competitive, we turn ourselves into the very monsters we were ostensibly fighting.

But I was not surprised to learn that Donald Trump would rather wallow in the gutter with ISIS than take the moral high ground.

Whenever I found myself surrounded by liars and cheats, I did not feel the temptation to become a liar and a cheat myself. On the contrary, I took greater pride in my honesty and integrity. Trump, with his win at any cost mentality, obviously was the opposite.

I found the worst part of Trump's interview with David Muir of ABC News was this. Rather than show leadership and direct his cabinet on the issue of whether or not to employ torture, Donald Trump said he would be content to allow his cabinet secretaries and advisors determine the policy. That was not leadership, it was the abdication of leadership.

If the Trump administration does employ waterboarding, no doubt they will follow the Bush administration's lead and claim that it would only be employed on hard core terrorists. And it may well start that way. But then once torture has begun to be employed, the temptation to use it more and more often grows stronger and stronger until the urge becomes overwhelming. This has proven to be true in every case where torture was employed. The definition of 'hard core terrorist' broadens until it encompasses just about everybody associated with the enemy, no matter how tenuously.

If torturing a terrorist might produce actionable intelligence, then perhaps torturing the terrorist's wife might work as well. Before you know it, you find that the CIA has begun to torture children. After all, that is precisely what happened when third world intelligence services employed torture.

But we Americans are better than they are, aren't we? Unfortunately, the results of the Stanford Prison Experiment and Stanley Milgram's experiments strongly suggest otherwise. We should never resort to torture under any circumstances. Not out of any concern for the wellbeing of the terrorists, they have already been corrupted beyond redemption, but for the mental health of our own intelligence officers. Another undeniable fact of torture is this. You cannot torture another human being without injuring your own psyche in the process.

44) Alternative Facts

According to Kellyanne Conway the members of the Trump administration never lie, they just utilize "alternative facts". I completely believe this. After all, the Trump administration functions in an alternative universe where Trump is the most popular president ever, who won by a landslide.

I can't help but wonder if Ms. Conway is feeling regret for having said that. This is something that is going to follow her for years to come. The way things are looking right now, "alternative facts" may well turn out to be the thing for which she will be most remembered. I'm not at all sure that I'd want that to be my legacy. But then again, such things often happen to people who serve a politician who is as wanton a liar as Donald Trump.

The worst part about this whole affair is that it wasn't even over anything important. Unlike Colin Powell, who sacrificed his credibility over the issue of whether or not Iraq had weapons of mass destruction, Ms. Conway's "alternative facts" concerned the attendance at Donald Trump's inauguration. Conway said it in defense of Press Secretary Sean Spicer who was claiming that Trump's inauguration was the most widely seen and attended inauguration in history.

Unfortunately for Mr. Spicer, photographic evidence demonstrated that the crowds on the National Mall for Trump's inauguration were a fraction of the size of the crowds attending Barack Obama's inaugurations, especially his first inauguration.

Of course, it is possible that many more people watched the inauguration on television or on the internet. It is even possible that people in Russia watched it in huge numbers. But that just begs the question: if the Trump administration is willing to blatantly lie about something as irrelevant as the attendance at Trump's inauguration, how can we trust them to tell us the truth about anything truly important?

That is not to say that an administration that always told the truth about petty issues can necessarily be trusted concerning the big issues. Hitler once said that the public would more readily believe a big lie than a small one. By big lie he meant a lie about an important issue. Consequently, the Nazi regime was often truthful about petty issues but almost always lied about the big issues. Big issues were always worth lying about while lies about petty issues just served to risk credibility without producing a corresponding political benefit. The Nazi regime was far more skilled at propaganda than the Trump Administration has been.

By displaying a willingness to lie about even the most petty and non-controversial of issues, the Trump administration has made it correspondingly more difficult to believe its pronouncements on the most important and controversial of issues.

45) The Limitations of Presidential Authority

Given Donald Trump's obvious penchant for autocratic management, it will be interesting to see what happens when he finally runs up against the limitations of presidential authority.

Donald Trump recently hosted a meeting of automobile industry executives at the Roosevelt Room of the White House during which he threatened to impose tariffs of automobiles assembled in Mexico. While Trump seemed quite pleased with this meeting, I'm wondering just how effective his threats could be. After all, no one attending that meeting with the possible exception of Trump himself believed that the President has the power to impose tariffs on imports.

Trump can't simply sign an executive order to impose such tariffs. Only Congress has the power to make the President's threat a reality. And Speaker of the House, Paul Ryan, has already stated that the Republican controlled Congress is very unlikely to do that.

Trump promised the auto executives that he would make the building and maintaining of assembly plants in the United States competitive. He intends to do this by relaxing environmental regulations and reducing taxation. But will this be enough? Won't he also have to relax health and safety regulations? And, most importantly, won't these new factories have to pay their workers less?

It will be interesting to see what really happens in the years ahead. Perhaps Trump is setting the Republicans in Congress up to take the blame if he proves unable to fulfill his campaign promises. Perhaps the Republicans will find that when Trump was calling for "draining the swamp" he was referring to them as well and not just the Democrats.

46) Dysphagia

I have been living with dysphagia for the last five years. Ever since undergoing a partial glossectomy to remove a cancer tumor from my tongue.

Dysphagia is a medical term for an inability to eat or swallow. As with many medical terms the word comes from the ancient Greek which literally means "not eating." Topic 32 explained the mechanics of swallowing and I will not repeat that material here.

For the last five years my diet has been limited to liquid nutrition and pureed food as I cannot swallow anything much thicker than the consistency of applesauce.

For the most part I was able to adapt to this new reality easily enough. I never was much of a gourmet. However, there have been times when I have missed being able to eat certain foods. Pizza and burgers are the foods I miss the most. At least, they seem to be the foods I most often wish I could eat again.

I also miss doughnuts. I tried to eat a doughnut once but I found I was not able to swallow it. Before my surgery I used to like to eat the little Tasty-Clair pies which Tastykake makes. I have tried to eat those again a couple times since my surgery but again, I was not able to swallow it. I thought that I would be able to eat the cream filling even if I could not eat the shell or the chocolate icing. I used a spoon to break open the shell and dig out the filling. I could spoon the filling into my mouth but I was not able to move it into my throat to swallow it.

I can eat chocolate but it is a slow process. I have to break off small pieces of chocolate and place them into my mouth. Then I would have to wait for the chocolate to melt before I could swallow it. Using this method it might take me an hour or two to eat a rather small piece of chocolate that most people could devour in a matter of minutes.

I can eat cheesecake and pumpkin pie. I can eat the filling if not the crust. While rather thick they are not too thick for me to force it through my mouth into my throat. While my tongue is tethered to the floor of my mouth it still has some mobility. Naturally, it does take me longer but not as long as eating a piece of chocolate.

I tried eating chili once but that turned out badly. I was able to swallow the smaller pieces. At least when I took my time. Unfortunately, I grew impatient and overly ambitious. I tried to swallow pieces that were too big and I tried to swallow them too quickly. I ended up choking on one piece. I think it was a piece of meat but it could have been a bean just as easily.

My attempt to swallow failed and the piece went into my trachea instead of my esophagus. It was not large enough to completely block my trachea but it did feel extremely uncomfortable. With a great deal of effort I was able to cough it back up. But the half minute during which I was coughing was one of the worst experiences of my life.

The fear of chocking to death took hold of me and it took every ounce of willpower I possessed to keep from panicking.

I have tried to eat bread but I found that I could not swallow it, not even in very small pieces. I tried eating a grilled cheese sandwich but I couldn't swallow that, either. I fixed myself French toast once, but I failed to cut the pieces up small enough and tried to eat it too quickly. I had trouble eating it and quickly gave up in frustration.

Now after five years I no longer feel sufficiently experimental to try anything else. But I might try again in the future, depending on whether or not I feel sufficiently daring. Until that time I will just have to remain content drinking Boost and smoothies. I used to eat a lot of applesauce, but I quickly grew tired of it. I might start eating it again, at least occasionally.

I used to eat quite a bit of ice cream and pudding as well. Unfortunately, I was diagnosed with type 2 diabetes. This diagnosis induced me to give up both ice cream and pudding as I needed to control my blood sugar and both ice cream and pudding are loaded with sugar.

Dysphagia may well be a blessing in disguise. Before my glossectomy my diet was not all that great. I used to eat fast food way too often and even when I did prepare my own food I probably did not always make the healthiest choices. I ate canned vegetables instead of fresh vegetables which meant that my sodium levels were probably too high. I also ate way too much snack food. Potato chips, cookies and cakes made up too much of my diet. But that realization does not make me miss potato chips and snack cakes any less. There have been plenty of times when I wished that I could indulge in my old habits.

But there is no turning back. I have had surgery to correct the tethering of my tongue but it was not successful. But as I've already observed, it's probably all for the best anyway.

47) Woody Allen Movies

I just finished watching *Vicky Cristina Barcelona*. It was definitely one of Woody Allen's best movies. One of the things I liked best about the movie was that Woody Allen was not in it. I feel that Woody Allen is a genius when it comes to writing and directing, but I have rarely been especially impressed with his acting. That is why the Woody Allen movies I have liked the best were the ones in which he did not personally appear.

Annie Hall didn't really appeal to me and I don't recall enough about the movie now to remember exactly why it didn't appeal to me. I just have this vague recollection that the movie was overrated. Well, that is just my opinion and what is that really worth? I'm not saying it was a bad movie, not at all. I'm just saying that I didn't think it was the best movie of 1977.

I thought Diane Keaton's performance in *Interiors* was far superior to her performance in *Annie Hall* despite the fact that she won the Oscar for best Actress for *Annie Hall* while her performance in *Interiors* did not even earn her an Oscar nomination. In fact, I thought that *Interiors* was a much better movie, but then again, Woody Allen wasn't in *Interiors* while he was the male lead in *Annie Hall*.

I'd like to point out here that I don't hate Woody Allen as an actor. There have been movies where his acting really added tremendously to the movie. *Zelig* was one such movie. His acting in *Bananas* was also superlative. As a matter of fact, Woody Allen has the distinction of being one of a very few actors who have ever elicited a laugh from me.

I feel that Allen's best performance as an actor came in *Stardust Memories*. But then, Allen was really playing himself and the movie was essentially a self parody, a subtle and brilliantly executed self parody.

The quality I most treasure in an actor is versatility. A great actor can convincingly play any type of personality. I guess my main complaint against Woody Allen's acting is that so many of the characters he portrays are interchangeable. They all seem to share the same personality.

I see the same quality in the characters portrayed by John Wayne which is why I never really took him very seriously as an actor. It is hard to admire an actor who played the exact same character in over two hundred different movies. The names and the circumstances might change but every one of John Wayne's characters shared the same basic personality.

48) Hypocrisy

Hypocrisy is one of the most common of human failings. It is usually born of rhetorical convenience. People like to win debates just as much as they like to win at any other competitive endeavor. Because of this trait people have a strong natural urge to employ whatever arguments appear to be the most effective whenever engaging in debates. They will criticize their opponents for failings which they themselves share or for engaging in activity which they themselves had indulged in. They will also sometimes even argue against their own positions if their opponent happens to be espousing that position at the time.

Politicians from both of the two major political parties do this all the time. But unlike private individuals who usually do not leave behind a record of their previous words and deeds, politicians have everything they say or do recorded somewhere. Speeches are videotaped and broadcast. Interviews are reported in the newspapers, on television and on the radio. Minutes record what the politicians say during meetings or on the floor of the House or Senate. Some of them even publish books.

All of these provide opportunities for politicians, who are after all professional debaters, to contradict themselves or otherwise set themselves up to become hypocrites.

People often notice the hypocrisy of politicians but for some strange reason they tend to only notice it when perpetrated by the politicians with whom they disagree. Thus people whose own political leanings align with the Republican Party tend to only notice the hypocrisy of the Democrats while those aligned with the Democratic Party tend to only notice the hypocrisy of the Republicans.

I certainly don't claim to be above this tendency. I find myself disagreeing with the Republicans more often than the Democrats and thus I more often notice the hypocrisy perpetrated by the Republicans. That is why I can more readily cite examples of Republican hypocrisy than I can Democratic examples.

The national debt offers a case in point. I noticed that the only times when the Republicans expressed any concern over the size of the national debt was when a Democrat occupied the oval office. Whenever a Republican was in the White House the national debt suddenly ceased to be a big issue. Just remember that it was Ronald Reagan who began the process of ballooning the national debt to astronomical heights. Nobody in the Republican Party complained while Reagan tripled the national debt in just eight years.

But the Republicans hardly hold a monopoly on hypocrisy. Democrat Nancy Pelosi has long been an advocate for resettling Syrian refugees in the United States, yet not a single Syrian refugee has been settled in the San Francisco Bay area which is the area which Ms. Pelosi herself represents in Congress.

I'm sure that the Democrats are just as guilty of taking both sides of the issue as the Republicans are. I just can't think of any examples off of the top of my head and I can't recall enough about any specific issues to make researching the subject worthwhile. All I can do now is resolve to pay closer attention in the future.

And the current size of the national debt is not the result of Republican policies alone. The Democrats have been just as guilty of pumping up that particular balloon over the years. When it finally bursts you can be sure that both parties will point the finger at the other. And you can be just as sure that both parties will be equally to blame.

49) Trump's Refugee Ban

On January 27th Donald Trump signed an executive order forbidding the citizens of seven specific countries from entering the United States for the next three months. This order also suspended the admission of refugees from those countries for four months and permanently prohibited refugees from Syria from entering the United States. The countries which Trump singled out for this treatment included Iran, Iraq, Syria, Libya, Yemen, Somalia and Sudan.

Here was a perfect example of the kind of incompetence I expected from the Trump Administration. The stated reason for this executive order was to prevent terrorists from entering the country. It's very title proclaimed it as such, but will it really do that? I doubt it. After all, how hard would it be for terrorists to obtain passports from other countries? Also, if Donald Trump was really interested to preventing terrorists from entering this country, then why didn't he include Saudi Arabia, Egypt, Afghanistan, Lebanon, the Palestinian Authority and Pakistan on the list of banned countries. After all, the men who carried out the 9/11 attacks were all from Saudi Arabia, the United Arab Emirates, Lebanon and Egypt but that didn't stop Trump from invoking 9/11 in his executive order.

No, obviously the executive order was not intended to protect America from terrorist infiltration, rather it was simply a measure to stop the flow of Muslim refugees. All seven of the listed countries were sources for refugees but how many terrorists have really come from there? As far as anyone knows, none.

An Iranian film received an Oscar nomination for Best Foreign Language Film but the filmmakers will not be able to attend the Academy Awards ceremony because of Trump's idiotic executive order. Furthermore, the order applied equally to all citizens of the targeted countries, even to those who were permanent residents of the United States.

And because Donald Trump was a "man of action and results" as Kellyanne Conway said the executive order went into effect immediately. This meant that people who were already in transit to the United States suddenly found themselves forbidden to enter the United States when they arrived. These people found themselves not only refused entry but detained at the airports.

Because of the excessive haste with which this executive order was executed no policies were formed for its implementation. State and local governments were not informed of this order in advance. A grace period was not included to forewarn people of this sudden change in policy. The hardships this policy would impose on people in transit were not even considered. I doubt that anyone in the Trump Administration would have cared anyway.

Trump's justification for this incompetent handling of his executive order was that if he gave advance warning of the change in policy then the "bad dudes" would all flock to the United States in the week before the policy was set to go into effect.

That has to be the most idiotic and specious explanation I have ever heard. None of the countries on the ban list were participants in the visa waiver program so the citizens of all of those countries would have to obtain a visa before being able to enter the country. It would be a simple matter to announce that no further visa applications would be accepted from those countries at the same time that the proposed travel restrictions were announced. That would be sufficient to prevent a flood of "bad dudes" from entering the country without the need to create hardships for travelers.

Unless the "bad dudes" he was worried about were people who already held visas. Now the lag time between the announcement of the new policy and the enforcement of that policy need not have been a week. It could have been a day or even just 12 hours. Whatever reasonable amount of time to ensure that people would not get caught in transit.

Naturally, this begged the question of just whom did Trump consider "bad dudes." Did he really believe that all Muslims were terrorists? That certainly seemed to be the implication of what he was saying. How could it be construed any other way?

Worse still this executive order was needlessly provocative. American prestige abroad has suffered a serious blow because of this ill conceived and ill implemented executive order. Trump obviously wanted to go back to the isolationist and protectionist policies of the 1930's. When the United States refused to admit refugees from Europe who wished to escape from Nazi oppression. That refusal to accept Jewish refugees played a large role in Hitler's decision to exterminate the Jews during World War II.

There already has been some backlash. Iran has promised to reciprocate. Some business leaders, especially in the high tech industry have spoken out against the executive order. Democrats have severely criticized Trump for this order, but such criticism was expected and likely to be completely ignored by their Republican colleagues.

The taxi drivers' union voted to refuse to pick up passengers from JFK airport in protest. Large crowds of protestors appeared at international airports in New York, Chicago, San Francisco, Washington, Boston, Dallas-Fort Worth, Denver, Houston, Los Angeles, Minneapolis-Saint Paul, Newark, Philadelphia, Portland, Salt Lake City, San Diego, Seattle-Tacoma and Boise to protest the executive order and demand that affected travelers be admitted into the country. The governor of Washington State, Jay Inslee, even held a press conference at the Seattle-Tacoma International Airport to voice his opposition.

The courts have also weighed in against Trump's executive order. Injunctions against enforcement of the order were issued by Judge Ann Donnelly of the Eastern District of New York, Judge Leonie Brinkema of the Eastern District of Virginia, Judge Thomas Zilly of the Western District of Washington and Judge Allison Burroughs of the District of Massachusetts.

None of these court orders weighed in specifically on the constitutionality of the order. They were merely intended as restraining orders to prevent people from being immediately removed from the country until the courts had the time to rule on the legality of the order.

Naturally, attorneys for travelers adversely affected by the executive order have not limited themselves to petitioning the courts for temporary stays and injunctions. They have also filed suits challenging the legality and constitutionality of the order. The states of Virginia, Washington, New York and Massachusetts have either joined in these lawsuits or initiated their own suits.

Several Washington based companies are assisting attorney general Bob Ferguson and Governor Jay Inslee in the state's lawsuit against Trump's immigration order. Microsoft, Amazon and Expedia have pledged their support for the legal action. Amazon and Expedia have filed declarations in federal court outlining the negative impact the order has had on their employees and their companies. Microsoft has promised to provide whatever testimony or evidence necessary to support the lawsuit.

In an interesting development, James Robart, the senior judge of the district court of the Federal District of Western Washington at Seattle, granted a temporary restraining order enjoining the Federal Government from enforcing Trump's refugee ban anywhere in the United States. This restraining order was granted after Nathaniel Gorton, a Federal District Judge in Boston, ruled in favor of Trump's order when petitioned for a restraining order against it by the American Civil Liberties Union.

The Trump Administration was not pleased with Judge Robart's decision. Press Secretary Sean Spicer, announced that the administration would appeal the ruling as quickly as possible. Trump himself deplored the decision and stated that he would hold the judiciary responsible for any terrorist acts committed after the ruling.

On February 9th the 9th Circuit Court of Appeals ruled unanimously to uphold the suspension of Trump's travel ban. Still claiming that national security was at stake, Trump has vowed to appeal to the Supreme Court. The Justice Department said that it was exploring its options.

Starbucks has pledged to hire 10,000 refugees. This has caused Trump supporters to call for a boycott of the company. They even started a social media campaign to drum up support for the boycott. However, it seems that this effort backfired. Opponents of Trump's order began a counter campaign and the boycott hashtag was soon displaced by hashtags favorable to Starbucks.

While there is no legal precedent for the courts overturning such an executive order, no other president had issued such a sweeping order, denying immigration benefits and visas to the inhabitants of an entire region. Previous travel restrictions had always been issued against only a single country and targeted narrowly defined groups or specific types of visas. No previous executive order banned entry to all of the citizens of a country or included legal permanent residents in such travel bans.

On February 2, hundreds of Yemeni Americans in New York City closed their shops in protest of Trump's immigration order. Beyond emphasizing the size of the Yemeni American community in New York I don't see this as more than a symbolic gesture at best. Clearly the only thing Trump himself cares about is his own political base.

It will be interesting to see what happens next. If the Trump Administration really does take this case to the Supreme Court the high court may well rule against them. Trump was certainly not doing himself any favors by making disparaging comments about the federal judiciary on Twitter.

50) The Electoral College

The electoral college is the only mechanism provided in the Constitution for electing the President and the Vice President of the United States. The way the government was designed by the Founding Fathers, the people were not supposed to vote for either the President or the Vice President. Rather they were supposed to trust electors chosen by the state legislatures to elect the President and Vice President on their behalf.

While the number of electors was determined by the Congressional representation in each state, the electors did not vote as a block. Each elector could vote for whichever candidate they chose, at least in theory. In practice, the electors were members of the two political parties and party discipline ensured that they voted for the candidates put forward by their respective parties.

The Founding Fathers hoped that through this system candidates for the highest offices in the land would be chosen on basis of qualifications rather than on the basis of popularity. The first five presidents, George Washington, John Adams, Thomas Jefferson, James Madison and James Monroe were elected under this system.

The popular vote was added by the state legislatures in the early 1820s in an effort to make the federal government more democratic. Perhaps it was a response to the fact that four out of the first five presidents were from Virginia. Perhaps it was because of the collapse of the Federalist Party coupled with the failure of the Independent Republican Party left America with only a single political party in 1824. Perhaps it was a response to the method by which presidential and vice presidential candidates were selected. Prior to the institution of primary elections party candidates were chosen by the Congressional caucuses of the two parties. The first presidential election featuring the popular vote was the Election of 1824.

It must be remembered that no candidate won enough electoral votes to win the presidency in 1824 so that was the first election decided by the House of Representatives. The House, voting on a state by state basis with each state having one vote, elected John Quincy Adams as President despite the fact that Andrew Jackson had won the most electoral and popular votes.

Jackson and his followers felt that he had been cheated. A feeling that deepened when the new President appointed the Speaker of House, Henry Clay, as his Secretary of State.

Back in 1825 the Secretary of State was regarded as the heir apparent to the Presidency rather than the Vice

President as up to that time more Secretaries of State won election to the presidency than Vice Presidents. Jackson surmised, probably correctly, that Adams had made a backroom deal with Henry Clay so that Clay would engineer his election by the House.

The reason why the state legislatures were able to introduce the innovation of the popular vote for President and Vice President was because the Constitution gave the state legislatures the power not only to choose their own electors but to determine the method by which they were chosen. Thus, the states were able to institute the popular vote and use it as the method for allocating their electoral votes. Once the popular vote had been implemented the actual appointment of electors became completely irrelevant as the electoral college became little more than a rubber stamp for the outcome of the popular vote.

So the winner of the popular vote should always win the electoral vote, right? Not necessarily. Since the only mechanism for electing the President provided for by the Constitution is the Electoral College, the Constitution only demands that a candidate win a plurality of the electoral votes to win the presidency. But with the states using the popular vote to determine the allocation of their electoral votes a strange quirk was added to the electoral process and Trump owes his election to that quirk.

By tying their electoral votes to the popular vote within the state, the state legislatures essentially changed the way their electors cast their votes. Before 1824 each elector cast his vote individually. After 1824 for most states all of the electoral votes were cast in a block for whichever candidate won the most popular votes in that state.

As the number of electoral votes in each state varies with the population of that state, the more populous states have more electoral votes than the less populous ones. This causes the votes of the people from the more populous states to have a greater weight in determining the outcomes of presidential elections than the votes of the people in the less populous states.

The Constitution gives to presidency to the candidate who wins 51% or more of the votes in the electoral college and with most of the states allocating their votes in a block to the candidate who wins the most votes in that state a candidate could win the presidential election by winning certain strategic states. Even if he wins those states by the margin of only a single vote. So a candidate can easily win the electoral vote while losing the popular vote simply by winning the popular in the most populous states.

The number of votes in the electoral college is equal to the number of Senators and Representatives in Congress plus three electoral votes for the District of Columbia. This gives a total of 538 electoral votes. To win the presidency, a candidate must win a plurality of the electoral votes or 271 out of 538.

This means that a candidate can win the presidency by winning just twelve states: California, Texas, New York, Florida, Illinois, Pennsylvania, Ohio, Michigan, Georgia, North Carolina, New Jersey and Virginia. The combined electoral votes of those 12 states equals to 283 votes, more than enough to secure the presidency. A candidate who wins all twelve of those states does not need to win a single vote from any other state and he only needs to win each of those particular states by one vote.

If third party candidates further divide the popular vote, it is quite possible for a candidate to win all twelve of the most strategic states while winning less than half of the popular vote of those twelve states. So it is possible for a candidate to win the presidency while winning only about 45% or 46% of the votes in only twelve states.

2016 and 1824 were not the only elections where the winning candidate did not win the popular vote.

Rutherford Hayes won the election of 1876 despite the fact that Samuel Tilden garnered more votes. In 1888 Benjamin Harrison also won the electoral vote while losing the popular vote.

But what really sets the 2016 election apart from the other elections was the margin by which Trump lost the popular vote. In the 1824, 1876 and 1888 elections the losing candidate's margin in the popular vote was only between 45,000 and 250,000 votes. In the 1824 election Andrew Jackson won only 44,804 more votes than John Quincy Adams. In 1876 Samuel Tilden's margin in the popular vote over Rutherford Hayes was 247,448 and Grover Cleveland's margin in the popular vote over Benjamin Harrison was 60,728. In the 2016 election Hilary Clinton won 2,868,520 more votes than Donald Trump.

Trump won 304 electoral votes to Clinton's 227. Seven electoral votes went to minor candidates. This means that Trump's margin of victory in the Electoral College was 33 votes. To appreciate just how close the election truly was consider that Pennsylvania has 20 electoral votes and Michigan has 16. Trump won Pennsylvania by a margin of 44,292 votes. He won Michigan by an even tighter margin, 10,704 votes. Had Trump not won both Pennsylvania and Michigan his total vote in the Electoral College would have been 268, not enough to win the election. This means that had trump won 54,996 fewer votes in those two strategic states, he would not have won the election.

I think electoral reform is needed but I don't think a constitutional amendment eliminating the Electoral College is necessary. Rather, I think the states need to simply amend their electoral laws to eliminate the winner take all method of awarding electoral votes. I think that electoral votes should be allocated in proportion to the popular vote. Thus, in an election like the 2016 Election where each candidate wins 50% of a state's popular vote then each candidate should receive 50% of the state's electoral votes. This would finally eliminate the strange quirk that allows the candidate who loses the popular vote to still win the election by winning the electoral vote.

51) Person of the Year

At the end of last year *Time* magazine named Donald Trump their "Person of the Year." While in any other context such a distinction would be a high honor, in this context it was not necessarily the case. The criterion which the editors of *Time* have historically used for naming their "Man" or "Person of the Year" was influence. The most influential person of the year was chosen to receive the distinction. Influence, however, can be bad as well as good and the people who have been named "Man" or "Person of the Year" in the past reflects this.

Pierre Laval was named "Man of the Year" in 1931. That year he was the Prime Minister of France as well as Minister of the Interior. In 1931 he was best known for his opposition to the Hoover Moratorium which suspended World War I debt payments, both principle and interest payments, for one year. Pierre Laval opposed the moratorium because it would halt German reparation payments to France. Laval was doubtlessly widely admired for this at the time because the Hoover Moratorium also saw strong opposition in the United States.

His later career was less than stellar. As Prime Minister and Foreign Minister in 1935, Laval presided over a secret meeting in Paris with the Italian League of Nations delegate, Pompeo Aloisi, and the British Foreign Secretary, Samuel Hoare. During this meeting Laval and Hoare agreed to allow Mussolini to conquer Ethiopia, the only sovereign state left on the continent of Africa.

After the German conquest of France in 1940 Laval served in the Vichy government, eventually rising to head of government in 1942. For this he was tried for treason after the war and executed in October, 1945.

Adolf Hitler was named "Man of the Year" in 1938. While Hitler was widely admired during the early years of his reign by 1938 he was clearly the world's biggest threat to international peace. Why he was not named "Man of the Year" again in 1939 I'm not sure, by any objective standard he was clearly the most influential figure for that year as well.

Time's "Man of the Year" for 1939 and 1942 was none other than Joseph Stalin. Doubtlessly the Soviet-German Non-Aggression Pact signed in 1939 was the reason for the Man of Steel receiving this "honor". That, and Soviet participation in the conquest of Poland. By 1942 the Soviet Union was an important ally and therefore was receiving nothing but positive press. The Russian victory over the Germans at Stalingrad was probably what earned Stalin his second "Man of the Year" award.

Mohammed Mossadegh was *Time's* "Man of the Year" in 1951. Mossadegh was the Prime Minister of Iran who nationalized the oil industry in that oil rich country. He was overthrown in a coup orchestrated by the CIA and MI 6 in 1953 and spent the rest of his life in prison.

The only other Iranian to receive *Time* magazine's "Man of the Year" was Ayatollah Khomeini in 1979. That year he overthrew the Shah of Iran and transformed Iran from a monarchy to an Islamic Republic. That was also the year Iranians seized the American embassy in Tehran and held the staff hostage.

"Man of the Year" for 1983 was shared by Ronald Reagan and Yuri Andropov. Andropov was the head of the KGB who succeeded Leonid Brezhnev as General Secretary of the Communist Party of the Soviet Union. In 1983 Soviet-American relations reached a dangerous low when the Soviet Air Force shot down Korean Airlines Flight 007. Among the passengers was a United States Senator.

Given the overall attitude of the mainstream press towards Donald Trump I strongly suspect that the editors at *Time* magazine regard him as a bad influence rather than a good one. I can't help but wonder, however, If Trump is proud of this "honor".

52) The National Security Council

In what is perhaps the most bizarre development in the increasingly bizarre Trump Administration, Donald Trump has reorganized the National Security Council. He removed both the Chairman of the Joint Chiefs of Staff and the Director of National Intelligence from the Principals Committee and replaced them with Steve Bannon, his chief advisor.

While Bannon is not entirely without qualifications, he did serve as an officer in the United States Navy for seven years and he did earn a Master's Degree in National Security Issues from Georgetown University, most of his professional life has been spent in movie production and media production. Admittedly, he is better qualified than Donald Trump to sit on the National Security Council but he can hardly be said to be better qualified than either the Chairman of the Joint Chiefs of Staff or the Director of National Intelligence.

The White House stated that the Chairman of the Joint Chiefs of Staff and the Director of National Intelligence would be invited to meetings of the Principals' Committee on a case by case basis when their specific expertise was wanted. But that just begs the question, when are the expertise of these two officials not needed when dealing with national security issues?

While it is true that George W. Bush also removed the Chairman of the Joint Chiefs of Staff and the Director of National Intelligence from the Principals Committee at the beginning of his first term, after the 9/11 attacks both men attended every meeting of the Principals Committee. So Bush's executive order made no difference in the formulation of national security policy.

While I don't have any problem with Donald Trump adding his top advisor to the committee, it seems to me that the removal of the Chairman of the Joint Chiefs and the Director of National Intelligence represented a serious error in judgment.

The question which undoubtedly will be answered in the immediate future is this: will Bannon's appointment to the Principals' Committee mean that his political influence will far outweigh professional judgment in the formulation of foreign and defense policy? I suspect that it will and I further suspect that we will see more bone-headed decisions from the White House in the coming months.

53) The European Union

I never thought I would live to see the day when the head of the European Union would regard the President of the United States as a threat to European wellbeing. Yet this is exactly what has happened. Donald Tusk, the President of the European Council recently sent a letter to the heads of the member states of the European Union listing the Trump Administration as one of the most serious threats now facing the European Union, along with Russia, China, terrorism, war and Islamic extremism.

How did we reach such a sorry state of affairs? Largely due to the asinine comments Trump has made both as a candidate for president and as President. He has maligned the NATO alliance and intimated that he might not feel obligated to honor the treaty. He has heaped praise on Vladimir Putin while simultaneously heaping criticism on German Chancellor, Angela Merkel. He has encouraged Britain to leave the European Union and expressed a desire to see the European Union disintegrate. He has even threatened in a recent interview with Michael Gove of the *Times* of London to issue travel restrictions on European citizens similar to the ones he recently imposed on certain Muslim countries. He has openly espoused protectionism as a way of "making America great again" and revived isolationist slogans from the 1930's, such as "America First".

54) Ukraine

Fighting has flared up in the eastern Ukraine between government forces and pro-Russian rebels. This is a war that has now been dragging on for three years. Ever since the deposing of Viktor Yanukovych in February, 2014. The Russians are blaming the Ukrainian government for this newest outbreak of fighting. They claim that the Ukrainians are trying to prevent the lifting of economic sanctions which the Obama administration had imposed after the forced annexation of the Crimea.

How long will it be before the Russians invade? What will Trump do? Probably nothing. He will probably regard a Russian invasion of the Ukraine as unimportant to American interests. And when the Russians invade will they just take back the eastern provinces or will they take back the entire country? I suspect that they will take the whole thing. The Ukraine has long been important to

Russia for its agriculture and natural resources. Far too important to allow its independence.

If I was Vladimir Putin, I would certainly do everything I could to engineer a return of the Ukraine to Russia and failing that at least to ensure as much Russian influence over that country as possible.

55) Fake News

Donald Trump stated during his Black History Month listening session that he didn't watch CNN because he didn't like fake news. I can understand and sympathize. After all, I don't like watching a fake President.

Trump has since announced that he will no longer allow anyone from his staff to be interviewed by CNN or any other news outlet that refuses to promote his agenda. I see this as a very positive development. Now the public has the rare opportunity to see which news outlets are legitimately interested in covering the news and which ones are more interested in being propaganda organs for the Trump Administration.

I wonder how long it will be before the only media outlets the Trump Administration will work with are Breitbart, Fox News and the *Washington Times*.

56) Suspension of Disbelief

Suspension of disbelief was an old theater term. It described the need for the audience to use their own imagination in order to accept as reasonable the patent absurdities which they often witnessed on the stage. For the sake of the story the audience had to accept that a large piece of papier-mâché was a fire-breathing dragon or that two actors swinging wooden props were engaged in a swordfight or that a handful of men on the stage represented the clash of mighty armies.

When the play was well written, well acted and well directed, suspension of disbelief was easy to achieve and maintain. When any of these three qualities was missing, then suspension of disbelief could be lost and the play fail to entertain.

Naturally, the closer to reality a stage play was the less imagination was need to appreciate it and consequently, the less suspension of disbelief was required to enjoy it. Thus plays grounded in the real world required less of a suspension of disbelief than plays that incorporated fantasy elements such as magic, monsters, ghosts or devils.

Suspension of disbelief wasn't just limited to stage plays. Any medium of storytelling could require it to a greater or lesser degree. Again, the degree to which suspension of disbelief was required depended on how far experiencing the story deviated from the audience's own expectations of reality.

Storytelling media that either more actively engaged the imagination, such as written or spoken stories, or media that presented their audiences with a more lifelike experience, such as motion pictures or television shows, required correspondingly less suspension of disbelief.

Because written and spoken stories more actively engaged the imagination of their audiences than more passive storytelling media they tended to require less suspension of disbelief. This was because the audience felt more immersed in the story whenever they read a story or heard a story told then they felt while watching a stage play, a movie or a television show.

Motion pictures and television shows required less suspension of disbelief than stage plays because they presented their audiences with a more lifelike experience. This was because the producers of a motion picture or a television show could employ hundreds or even thousands of extras to represent an army instead of relying on a handful of actors. Photographic effects and special effects available to motion picture and television cinematographers gave Motion picture and television props a far more realistic appearance than can be given the props of a stage play.

Since believability is the key determinant in the amount of suspension of disbelief a story required of its audience, the genre of the story also played a significant role in determining the degree of suspension of disbelief required by that story. Since science fiction and fantasy were far more divorced from reality than the other genres. They required more of a suspension of disbelief from their audiences

Everyone's capacity for suspension of disbelief varied. So I suspected that people who did not like either science fiction or fantasy were not capable of the requisite suspension of disbelief necessary to enjoy those types of stories. This may well explain why some people don't enjoy stage plays, for that matter.

I can sustain a rather high degree of suspension of disbelief. But even more capacity is not infinite. I recently saw a movie that demanded more of a suspension of disbelief than I was willing to provide.

This movie was *The Water Horse*, a New Zealand, British, and Australian co-production made in 2007. The movie told the story of a Scottish boy who befriended the Loch Ness Monster.

I was willing to accept the basic premise of the story at face value. Where I balked was near the end of the movie where the boy, who could not swim, was shown clinging to the creature's back while it engaged in rapid and complex swimming maneuvers underwater.

I could accept the existence of the creature. I could even accept the emotional bond between the creature and the boy. What I could not accept was the idea that a boy who could not swim and consequently had a healthy reluctance to enter the water would really so readily jump onto the creature's back. But even if he was a champion swimmer with no fear of the water I did not believe that he could really stay on the creature's back while it carried out the maneuvers shown in the movie. Furthermore, the creature seemed to remain submerged for absurdly long periods of time. So long, in fact, that I would have expected the boy to drown.

57) Imperialism and the Profit Motive

When Donald Trump visited CIA headquarters the day after his inauguration he gave a speech where he said that it was a serious mistake that the United States did not seize control of Iraq's oil reserves. This blunt advocacy of imperialism was abnormal, even by Trump's strange standards. But it makes sense from his point of view.

After all, Trump is no statesman. He is a businessman with absolutely no political experience whatsoever and the sine qua non of businessmen is the profit motive. Everything a businessman does is intended, either directly or indirectly, to increase his firm's profitability. Even a company's charitable donations are intended to build goodwill with an eye towards increasing future profits.

So, it can be no surprise that Trump always thinks in terms of profit and loss when making decisions. Good decisions are those which generate profit. Bad decisions are those that incur loss. Morality plays no role in this. Neither does any other consideration. Profit and loss are the only valid criteria.

There are two ways of increasing profits. The first way is by increasing revenue. The second way is by decreasing cost. The best businessmen do both at the same time. Trump clearly regards himself as one of the best businessmen, therefore he clearly intends to do both and this is the pattern that will doubtlessly become established by his administration.

His executive order freezing government hiring was obviously a cost saving measure. His travel ban was most likely a cost saving measure as well. If you don't allow people from 'dangerous' countries into the country then you don't need to perform expensive background research or surveillance. If you block refugees then you eliminate the costs involved in bringing refugees into the country and helping them become established here.

He wants to build a wall along the southern border at a cost of $15-20 billion but he is insistent that the Mexicans pay for it. Passing on the cost to someone else is another excellent way to minimize your own costs and maximize your own profits. This was the same motivation for his repeated us of Chapter 11 Bankruptcy when managing his businesses.

In the coming months he will doubtlessly attempt to get America's allies to pay for the presence of American military units abroad. This will be especially interesting to see in the case of Cuba. Are the Cubans going to be willing to pay for Guantanamo Bay?

Note that I'm not just talking about covering the cost of those units, I'm talking about making a profit from those deployments. Trump himself has hinted at this without going into enough detail to make his plan clear. How many of our allies will be willing to do that?

Seizing Iraq's oil reserves makes perfect sense if your concept of "making America great again" means operating the federal government on a for profit basis. It makes perfect sense if your foreign policy is geared towards generating revenue instead of promoting freedom.

Just remember, though, running foreign policy for the sake of generating profit is the heart and soul of imperialism.

58) Nativism

The Washington Post has recently acquired copies of two proposed executive orders drawn up by the Trump Administration. Both of these orders deal with immigration.

The first is titled "Executive Order on Protecting Taxpayer Resources by Ensuring Our Immigration Laws Promote Accountability and Responsibility." This executive order would call upon specific standards to be developed for determining whether immigrants are likely to become public charges or have become public charges within their first five years of residency.

Once these standards have been developed they are to be used to deny admission to foreigners that fall within those standards. Also, any immigrant who receives welfare assistance would be deported if the amount of that assistance is sufficiently high to meet the new standards of becoming a public charge.

This executive order does not really represent a change in law as the existing laws already provide for the denial of residency to immigrants deemed likely to become a public charge. Currently, immigrants are required to have a sponsor and that sponsor must demonstrate sufficient income to support the immigrant. Furthermore, the sponsor must sign a contract with the federal government promising to provide support for the immigrant. What this executive order would change is the vigor with which the federal government seeks to enforce these laws.

Currently, once the decision is made to admit an immigrant there is no mechanism to follow the immigrant and ensure that he or she has not become a public charge since admission. Trump's proposed executive order would change that.

While more vigorously enforcing the existing laws seems reasonable enough on the surface, overly strict enforcement would create more problems than it would solve. Overly vigorous enforcement of the law could penalize recent immigrants unfairly for circumstances completely beyond their control.

One potential problem, of course, is that situations can change with surprising rapidity. A person with a well-paying job can suddenly find themselves unemployed through no fault of their own. I found my own income cut in half this way when I was stricken with cancer.

Also, most legal immigrants don't just come over here alone. Most enter the country as the spouses of American citizens. So, most legal immigrants live in households which also contain American citizens. Should a legal immigrant really be deported because his or her family fell on hard times? Also consider that just because someone is on welfare at one time doesn't necessarily mean that they will stay on welfare forever.

Given the unthinking and uncaring way that Trump's executive order on immigration was carried out, I expect that this executive order would be carried out in the same way, without any regard for the hardships imposed on individual families.

The second proposed executive order is titled "Executive Order on Protecting American Jobs and Workers by Strengthening the Integrity of Foreign Worker Visa Programs." This order calls for the revocation of work visas that were issued contrary to American immigration laws, which is fine on the surface of it. If a visa is obtain fraudulently then it shouldn't be valid. But it also calls for the revocation of work visas deemed to be "contrary to national interest." That seems to me to be giving the government carte blanche to revoke at will any work visa from any hapless immigrant that some government bureaucrat deems to be 'stealing' a American job.

It is obvious that Trump has an anti-immigrant agenda which he is trying to implement slowly. This policy clearly seeks to first limit new immigrants from entering the country and then deport as many existing immigrants as legally possible. I'm sure if Trump could have his way he would forbid all immigration and deport all immigrants.

Taken together, these two proposed executive orders are clearly a nativist assault on immigration itself. Nativism is nothing new to this country. It has been around since 1844 when Irish immigrants began coming to this country in droves during the Irish Potato Famine.

Back then religion was the main reason for the rise of nativism as well. The Irish immigrants who came to escape poverty and famine in the native land were predominantly Catholic. Nativism from the 1840's was geared towards keeping the Catholics out while Trump's own 21st century revival is obviously intended to keep out the Muslims.

So Trump intends to increase American jobs by kicking out the immigrants. Interesting. Especially when you consider that two out of his three wives are immigrants. One could easily make the case that these wives were stealing 'jobs' away from native Americans when they married Donald Trump. Personally, I wouldn't go so far, but I still consider it the height of hypocrisy.

I suspect that the only reason that these two executive orders have not already been signed and put into effect was because of the unexpected backlash his executive order stopping refugees and immigrants from seven Muslim countries. I believe Trump had expected enthusiastic support for his refugee ban and was genuinely taken aback when he didn't get it. Perhaps signing the refugee ban will be as far as Trump's nativist agenda will come to full implementation. We can only hope.

59) University of California at Berkeley

At the University of California at Berkeley the extreme left insisted on proving that they are every bit as stupid and hypocritical as the extreme right. Simply protesting the appearance of right wing extremist, Milo Yiannopoulos, at the liberal campus was not good enough for these knuckleheads. They had to resort to violence to prevent the man from speaking.

Freedom of speech is completely meaningless if it does not include everyone. Especially if it does not include those with whom we disagree. This was well understood by Evelyn Hall who famously wrote in *Friends of Voltaire*, "I disapprove of what you say but I will defend to the death your right to say it." The only thing the hooligans at Berkeley accomplished was to devalue and delegitimize their own position.

The best way to deal with people like Yiannopoulos is to let them speak. Extremists like him usually have such a penchant for overstating their positions that they often undermine themselves. Every time one of these people speaks he runs the risk of saying something foolish or taking a position that may later prove inconvenient. That's why it is important to allow them to speak. And equally important to record what they say. By closing down the event and preventing Yiannopoulos from speaking, the protesters eliminated those possibilities. Just remember that the first man to translate *Mein Kampf* into English, Edgar Dugdale, was a Zionist.

Trump's threat to defund the university for this is yet another example of a thoughtless knee-jerk reaction from him. At present it is not clear exactly who were responsible for the rioting or whether the university could have done anything to prevent it. Until these things are known any action against the university would be premature.

60) The Bowling Green Massacre

Have you ever heard of the Bowling Green Massacre? I haven't. I even performed a Google search to see if it was an event that had somehow escaped my notice at the time. I don't always follow the news assiduously. But an internet search produced nothing. The Bowling Green Massacre turned out to be nothing more than another one of Kellyanne Conway's "alternative facts", a deliberate falsehood meant to justify the Trump Administration's immigration policies.

Mohanad Shareef Hammadi and Waad Ramadan Alwan had entered the United States as refugees in 2009 and settled in Bowling Green, Kentucky. In 2011 the FBI learned that they had been insurgents who had planted improvised explosive devices along roadsides in Iraq. Upon arrest the two men admitted to carrying out terrorist activities against American forces in Iraq which included detonating IEDs against American troops resulting in the deaths of American soldiers.

While in America Hammadi and Alwan were engaged in obtaining weapons and raising money for Al-Qaeda. But they did not engage in terrorist acts within the United States, much less commit a massacre in their adopted hometown. Hammadi and Alwan were both convicted. Hammadi is serving a life sentence while Alwan is serving forty years.

Kellyanne Conway has since tweeted that she misspoke when she claimed that there had been a massacre at Bowling Green. Rather, she was referring to the arrest and conviction of Hammadi and Alwan. Ah, but when she was talking the MSNBC's Chris Matthews didn't she claim that the public was unaware of the 'massacre' because the media refused to cover it? Wasn't that supposed to be her whole point? ABC did cover the arrest and conviction of Hammadi and Alwan. She even included a link in her tweet to the ABC story. The Trump Administration has no credibility and Conway's attempts to give it credibility have caused her to sacrifice her own.

61) South Park

The creators of *South Park*, Trey Parker and Matt Stone, have announced that they will stop, at least temporarily, satirizing Donald Trump on their animated television show. The stated reason for this decision was that "satire had become reality." I suspect that this means that Trump has been doing such a great job making himself look ridiculous that satirizing him has become redundant.

I have never watched *South Park* myself. I've always found their particular brand of humor too crude for my tastes. As far as that goes, I'm not a big fan of comedy in general. So much comedy relies on being ridiculous to make a point and I don't honestly have much of a taste for the ridiculous. I much prefer subtle humor and *South Park* has never been subtle.

62) How the Trump Administration Might End

There are several possible ways that the Trump Administration might come to an end. The most obvious and probably the most likely scenario is that Donald Trump simply serves out his term of office. I think it is highly unlikely that Trump will be re-elected in 2020, so four years is the longest life expectancy for the Trump Administration.

The second possibility is that Trump is assassinated. While I personally hope that this not happen, it is a distinct possibility. Especially with Trump going after Al-Qaeda and ISIS the way that he is. That coupled with all of the discontent his administration has generated so far. I have never seen a president alienate so many people so quickly before. So, Trump could become a target for assassination, either by foreign terrorists or domestic malcontents.

The third possibility is impeachment. I am doubtful of this possibility, especially with the Republicans in control of the House and the Senate. But two things could happen which might make this a stronger possibility. The Democrats could regain control of the House or Senate in 2018 or Trump could alienate the Republican Congressional leadership sufficiently that they decide to get rid of him.

The fourth possibility is one that no one seems to be considering yet, Trump could simply resign. He might decide that he has had enough of the constant and harsh criticism or he might realize that he is not the right man for the job. But I think the most likely reason for a resignation would be if he realized that being President of the United States was harming his personal business, especially the value of his personal brand. Evidence for an erosion of the value of that brand is already appearing. Both Nordstrom's and Neiman Marcus have dropped Ivanka Trump's clothing and jewelry lines. There is also a grassroots movement underway to boycott stores which carry any of Trump's personal brands or those of his immediate family.

The fifth possibility is another one that no one seems to consider, possibly because most pundits are unaware of the possibility. Trump could be removed by his own cabinet due to mental instability.

Section 4 of the Twenty-Fifth Amendment provides that "Whenever the Vice President and a majority of either the principal officers of the executive department or of such other body as Congress may by law provide, transmit to the President pro tempore of the Senate and the Speaker of the House of Representatives their written declaration that the President is unable to discharge the powers and duties of his office, the Vice President shall immediately assume the powers and duties of the office of Acting President."

Naturally, the President could attempt to regain his office by written declaration that he is able to perform his duties, but this could simply lead to the Vice President and the cabinet to again declare him unfit. Then Congress would have to decide the issue.

Could Trump become the first President in history to be removed from office as mentally unfit? He seems sufficiently erratic to at least make this a tantalizing possibility. Seems highly improbable, but then again, so did his election.

63) The Individual Mandate

The one part of the Affordable Care Act that I really disliked was the individual mandate. I really thought that it was grossly unfair for the federal government to mandate that people purchase health insurance and to fine people for non-compliance.

The Obama Administration compared the individual mandate to the requirement for car owners to purchase automobile insurance. The problem is that people choose to own automobiles and people are legally free to choose not to own an automobile. People do not choose to be alive and the law does not permit people to choose to die.

The strangest aspect of the individual mandate was how it was enforced. The Obama Administration chose to use the Internal Revenue Code to enforce the individual mandate. The fine for non-compliance was imposed upon the tax return of the non-compliant individual. This meant that those who did not have to file income tax returns could not be fined. This essentially exempted the poorest Americans from compliance from a law that was supposedly designed to ensure that the poorest Americans had access to health insurance.

I had health insurance through my employer last year. The deductible was so high that the plan paid very little of my healthcare costs for the year. I paid out of my pocket for most of my healthcare while simultaneously paying biweekly premiums. This situation did not impress me and I would have dropped the health insurance were it not for the individual mandate.

64) Self Loathing and Denial

During yesterday's broadcast of *Real Time* with Bill Maher the host discussed the problem of militant Islam with guest Sam Harris. During this discussion the two cited liberal self loathing as contributing to the problem. Now I know that liberal self loathing is a very real phenomenon. I have personally seen it in action.

In 1985 during the 40th anniversary of the bombing of Hiroshima I saw a news program covering the observance of the anniversary in Hiroshima. The news broadcast featured an American girl in tears over how the United States could have ever perpetrated such an atrocity. That was the perfect example of liberal self loathing in action.

The girl seemed to be under the impression that the United States Air Force just woke up that morning and

133

decided to drop an atomic bomb on Hiroshima just for the hell of it. Like it was just another bomb test like the ones done on Bikini Atoll. No mention of the fact that the United States and Japan were at war at the time.

I don't want to minimize the horrors experienced by Japanese civilians in Hiroshima. But the bombing of any city is a horrible experience for the civilians who endure it. The Japanese certainly bombed their fair share of cities during the war, Shanghai and Nanjing in particular suffered horribly. The only reason that American cities did not suffer this same destruction was simply because the Axis powers lacked the means of delivering it. Both the Germans and the Japanese would have happily leveled every city in America if they could have.

I agree that the bombing of Hiroshima and Nagasaki were horrible and I also agree that the bombing of Tokyo was equally horrible. But I also feel the same way about the bombing of Shanghai, Nanjing and Chongqing. I feel that war in general is a horrible business which we should avoid as much as possible. Unfortunately, I also recognize that circumstances sometimes render that impossible. That's why I don't feel guilty about it. America didn't start the war, we just finished it.

I think that we need to learn from the mistakes of our ancestors lest we continue to perpetrate them. But I don't believe in racial guilt. For me to feel guilty over what was done decades before I was even born is as stupid as me feeling guilty over a crime which I did not commit just because the perpetrator was a white guy. So I never buy into liberal self loathing.

But by the same token I don't buy into conservative denial. Conservatives all too often buy into the myth that discrimination is dead and buried just because it is illegal, that it doesn't occur because it is no longer practiced openly. The KKK may not be as large or as powerful as it once was but it is still here.

While it is obvious that liberalism hasn't eliminated black poverty, it is equally obvious that conservatism hasn't either. Whatever the solution to that particular problem is it clearly has not been tried yet. And the reason for that is the sad fact that the liberals persist in trying the same failed policies while the conservatives persist in denying the existence of the problem altogether.

Or perhaps more accurately the conservatives deny any responsibility for solving the problem. Which brings me to another interesting phenomenon. Republicans complain that black voters won't vote for them. But is that any surprise when the Republicans steadfastly ignore the issues confronting black Americans? So we have this chicken and egg conundrum. The Republican Party largely ignores the issues of the black community because the black community will not vote for them while the black community won't vote for Republican candidates because they ignore the issues of the black community. The situation is really just another part of conservative denial, the complaint about black voting habits is really just an excuse. The Republicans want to run the country and running the country means dealing with all of the nation's problems, not just the ones with which they want to deal.

65) Deregulation

It is a central tenet of conservatism that the only road to prosperity is allowing the business community to have as unfettered a hand as possible when conducting their business. The conservatives tell us that business leaders are experts in their fields and are thus better qualified to manage their concerns than are government bureaucrats. They tell us that regulation of businesses is best left to market forces rather than to government decrees. The conservatives claim that market forces coupled with enlightened self-interest do a much better job at regulating the conduct of business than anything the government could do.

This is certainly an appealing ideology and one which once was valid. In the good old days when businesses were small and local and ownership was not independent of management, the conservative ideology certainly held a great deal of validity. Bankers and business owners lived within the communities where they did business. Everyone knew them. They were pillars of the community. The businessman who made a habit of cheating his customers or his employees did not stay in business very long. Back then business transactions themselves were simple enough for most people to understand. Everyone knew when they were cheated.

Today business is dominated by a handful of massive multinational corporations. Whole industries are completely controlled by them. With the rise of the corporation came two simultaneous developments. The first is the rise of professional management. With professional management came the divorcement of management and ownership. The second development was the increasing complexity of business transactions. It has now reached the point where one has to have an advanced degree in accounting to understand business transactions.

Now an increasing number of businesses are no longer local. Their owners and managers are no longer members of the community. In fact, the owners and managers are not even the same people any more. And with the increased complexity of business it has become increasingly difficult for the consumer to know when he's being cheated.

With the rise of professional management money has become the measure of all things. Success in business is measured in terms of profit and loss which are in turn measured in terms of money gained or lost. The performance of professional management is measured in profit and loss. This alone would provide sufficient motivation for fraud but this is coupled with the fact that ownership is now divorced from management and the owners are only in it for the money.

These circumstances lead to an intense and constant pressure on management to increase profitability. For the professional management class both their own economic wellbeing and their egos are predicated upon the profitability of the firms under their control. Maximizing profit becomes their raison d'être. Naturally, they will maximize their profits ethically as much as possible. But if ethics get in the way of profitability then it is always ethics which are cast aside. In a similar vein they will maximize profits legally as much as possible, but again, when legality gets in the way then it is legality which is cast aside.

That is why regulation and the vigorous enforcement of those regulations are critically important. When it comes down to it the only thing which the massive multinational business concerns can be relied upon to do is to pursue the maximization of profits. They cannot be trusted to act either ethically or legally in the pursuit of those profits.

The reason for this is simple enough, greed always trumps good judgment. This has been shown to be true over and over again. Business leaders have been willing to do some of the most incredibly foolish things for the sake of quick profits. They will drive their own businesses into insolvency and bankruptcy if they can make a quick fortune. This is especially true if they can escape from the wreckage of their failed firms through golden parachutes.

Whoever thought slavery was a good idea? Nobody. Even the staunchest defenders of the institution of slavery regarded it as a 'necessary evil'. They were half right. It was certainly an evil but clearly not a necessary one. Oh, but the money that was made on the backs of the slaves!

Half of the economy of the United States was based on a cash crop economy supported by slave labor. A third of the inhabitants of the ante bellum South were slaves. So strong was the grip of the slavery addiction on the South that it required the bloodiest war in American history to break it. We are paying the price for that particular brand of foolishness to this very day.

Who thought it was a good idea to cram the cargo holds of merchant ships with slaves as though they were sardines in a can? Nobody. Slaves died on each voyage. Some of those who didn't die were permanently weakened by the experience. So disgusted was the American public with the transatlantic slave trade that all Americans, even the Southerners, agreed to abolish it. Oh, but the slave traders made fortunes while it lasted.

Who thought it was a good idea to sell stock at ten percent margin? Obviously Wall Street bought into this foolishness. A lot of money was made for as long as the bubble lasted. Even the commercial banks started to get in on the action, buying stock with depositors' money instead of issuing loans. Then the bubble burst, investors couldn't cover their margins and the commercial banks began falling like dominoes.

The stock market crash of 1929 is the kind of thing that happens when greed trumps good judgment. It is the kind of thing that happens when the Republicans control the House, the Senate and the White House and refuse to regulate the business community. And it happens every time the Republicans gain complete control over the federal government.

The Republicans gained control in the 1980's and deregulated the savings and loan industry. This quickly resulted in the mismanagement of savings and loans which in turn led to some of them failing spectacularly.

The Republicans gained control again in the early years of this century and we were treated to yet another spectacular failure brought about by the failure of the government to regulate business. This time the investment banks began to collapse. Lehman Brothers and Bear Sterns did collapse. Goldman Sachs and Merrill Lynch only survived because Congress and the Bush Administration bailed them out.

At the time I thought that the investment bank bailout was the proper thing to do. Now I wonder if perhaps the government should have just let them fail. That certainly would have been the conservative thing to do. If government insists on allowing the business community to do whatever it wants they should also allow the business community to suffer the consequences. Isn't that the best way to instill a sense of responsibility in business leaders.

Now in 2017 the Republicans find themselves in control of the House, the Senate and the White House again. And again, they are deregulating the business community. They claim that this will spark prosperity, but if the past is any indication of what is likely to happen, then I expect to see another financial crisis involving one of the deregulated industries. Greed always trumps good judgment.

66) A Stark Contrast

In justifying his completely unjustifiable travel ban, Donald Trump had the temerity to claim that his executive order was very similar to an executive order issued by Barack Obama in 2011. Obama's executive order did not generate the controversy that Trump's order generated so the public doubtlessly was largely unfamiliar with it. I imagine that Trump was counting on this unfamiliarity to allow the public to accept his rather facile claim at face value. Unfortunately for Trump, the press routinely checks the accuracy of claims such as his and it didn't take the press long to determine the falsity of Trump's claim.

The Obama administration's immigration actions were prompted by the FBI's discovery in 2011 that two Iraqi Al-Qaeda militants had entered the United States as refugees in 2009. Obama's executive order halted admission of refugees and also halted the issuing of special visas to Iraqi's for six months while more thorough vetting methods were developed and implemented. Note that this executive order only applied to Iraq while Trump's order targeted seven countries. Also, Obama's order fell far short of being a travel ban. The issuing of tourist and business visas was not affected by the order. Trump's order, on the other hand, stopped the issuance of all types of visas except diplomatic visas.

It is also important to note that Obama's order was prompted by a specific and credible threat. What threat prompted Trump's order? Nothing. The only thing which prompted Trump's order was the President's own xenophobia coupled with a desire to demonstrate to his political base that he was a "man of action and results."

Another difference between the Obama order and the Trump order was that the Obama order was not rushed out without consulting the relevant executive departments. Its implementation was not accompanied by the confusion and heartache experienced from the implementation of Trump's order. There were no reports of travelers being caught in midair by the order. No reports of people being detained or deported at the airports.

Perhaps one of the most bizarre aspects of the Trump Administration's justification for the travel ban is the claim that the Obama Administration had chosen the seven countries on the travel ban. Really? Seriously? They were in such a hurry to throw out this executive order that they couldn't even develop their own list? They seriously had to rely on the Obama Administration to tell them where the terrorists were coming from? And they would just accept that without trying to verify it first?

While I have no doubt at all that the Obama Administration regarded those seven countries with concern considering the political chaos in most of them, I strongly suspect that the Trump Administration is once again employing "alternative facts" to turn apples into oranges. Saying that one is "concerned" about certain countries is not the same as saying that those countries are actively exporting terrorism.

The executive order itself cited the 9/11 attacks as its justification. Then the very countries from which the 9/11 terrorists came were not included in the travel ban. Makes me wonder two things. Who wrote this order and would Trump have signed it if Saudi Arabia and Egypt had been included?

Despite its title and its claim, Trump's travel ban was obviously inspired by nativism and designed to halt the admission of refugees. Obviously the nations were chosen not because they were hotbeds of terrorism but because they were the main sources of refugees. But a ban on terrorists obviously has a much better chance of passing legal muster than a ban on refugees.

67) Going Way Too Far

I have always been a strong supporter of the people's First Amendment rights to protest and petition the government. This has long been one of the most important rights guaranteed by the United State Constitution. However, like all such rights, they are not without their limitations. I support any and all protests provided that they remain peaceful and are not carried out contrary to the law.

While people have the right to protest, they do not have the right to vandalize property, assault those who disagree with them, trespass, prevent businesses or government offices from operating or block public streets. Unfortunately, we see protestors all too often refuse to abide by these restrictions. We have seen this in some of the recent protests. Buildings have been vandalized and automobiles have been set on fire. Some protests have devolved into full scale riots.

These things happen because protestors often feel very strongly about the issue which they are protesting and more often than not protests are largely ignored by both the government and the public at large. Frustration at the failure of their message to make an immediate impact sometimes causes the protestors to cross the line of acceptable behavior.

A case in point was the recent protest over Trump's travel ban carried out in New Haven, Connecticut. It wasn't enough for the protestors to simply voice their opposition to the travel ban, they had to block New Haven streets as well. They even went so far as to block I-95 at the Exit 47 ramp.

Connecticut State troopers were called in to clear the highway but they were not able to prevent the protestors from keeping an ambulance from transporting a critically ill person to the hospital. Because the protestors stopped the ambulance, the ambulance crew was forced to perform emergency procedures on the patient.

Is protesting Trump's travel ban really worth placing a person's life at risk? I don't think so. In fact, the organizer of that protest has been taken into custody. Fortunately for him the patient did not die. While the organizer certainly could not be charged criminally for the patient's death, he could be held civilly liable. This means that while the organizer could not go to jail for the patient's death, he could be sued for a substantial amount of money. Wrongful death suits can be very expensive.

Once again we bear witness to another group of protestors whose inability to contain their actions to within acceptable norms serves to undermine the cause which they seek to promote.

68) The Cost of Doing Business

One of Donald Trump's campaign promises was that he would not accept his presidential salary. He would only accept a dollar a year in pay while President. His supporters then gleefully calculated that his presidency would only cost the American taxpayers $8. Of course that assumed that he would be re-elected in 2020, a prediction which shows all the signs of being premature. It also ignores the fact that the cost of maintaining the President includes far more expenses than just his salary.

Presidential travel and Secret Service protection also costs money. And those travel and security expenses apply to more than just the President himself. The government also pays the travel and security expenses for the members of the President's immediate family.

Donald's son, Eric, made a two day business trip to Uruguay near the beginning of last month. The government paid for the hotel accommodations as well as other expenses for the Secret Service security team which accompanied him. It is standard practice for the Secret Service to provide security for the immediate family of a President-elect.

The cost for all this to the American taxpayer was $97,830. While I am not trying to suggest that previous Presidents did not incur similar expenses, I am suggesting that Trump was being disingenuous when he claimed that his Presidency is only going to cost the taxpayers a $1 a year.

69) Sacrifice and Baptism

Most people are familiar enough with the life and career of Jesus of Nazareth to know that he had been baptized by John the Baptist in the River Jordan. But what was the true significance of that event?

John the Baptist himself claimed that his baptisms would grant spiritual absolution to whoever underwent the ritual. This was quite a radical claim at the time. Baptism was a ritual which had been practiced by the Jews since the time of Moses but it was not used to grant absolution from sins. Rather, baptism was a purification ritual intended to remove spiritual uncleanliness such as that which resulted from menstruation, contact with ejaculate or contact with a dead body.

In traditional Judaism sin could only be expiated through a sin offering given at the temple. The Old Testament gave detailed regulations on what kind of animal was to be sacrificed and on how that sacrifice was to be performed. Devout Jews were expected to make a sin offering every time they knowingly committed a sin. The ancient Jews recognized that men could sin without realizing it. Thus they instituted the practice of making a sin offering every year on the Day of Atonement. This sin offering was supposed to cover those sins which had been committed unconsciously.

In the days of Moses the Jews were a pastoral people. Just about everyone had their own flocks and herds from which to obtain sacrificial animals and those few who did not would easily have access to suitable animals. But by the temple period things had changed. The Jews had settled down and become farmers and city dwellers. Many did not own their own flocks and herds and many more no longer had access to suitable sacrifices.

The temple solved this particular problem by maintaining its own flocks and herds from which it could sell sacrificial animals to those who did not have livestock of their own.

By the time of Jesus Judea had become a province of the Roman Empire. As such the coins used in everyday commerce were minted by the Roman authorities.

Remember the debate Jesus had with the Pharisees concerning whether it was permitted for devout Jews to pay the Roman taxes. Jesus responded by asking whose coins they carried in their pockets. When the Pharisees admitted that their coins were Roman Jesus replied that this fact made it permissible for the Jews to pay the Roman taxes. After all, their money already belonged to the Romans.

Now the temple authorities decided that Roman coins could not be used to purchase sacrificial animals from the temple. Doubtlessly this doctrine was derived from the fact that the Roman coins bore the images of the Roman Emperors upon them. Since the Roman Emperors were worshipped as gods, the Jewish priests regarded them as ritually unclean and therefore unfit for use in purchasing sacrificial animals.

Again, the temple came up with a solution to this dilemma. Money changers affiliated with the temple would set up tables in the outer courtyard where they would exchange the unclean Roman currency for clean temple shekels. The Jews could then use the shekels to purchase their sacrificial animals.

These were the same money changers whose tables Jesus overturned in the temple. The same men he denounced for turning his father's house into a den of thieves. Jesus' reaction was doubtlessly triggered by the fact that the money changers must have been making a profit from the exchanges. Thus, they and the priests were profiteering from God's holy rituals.

John the Baptist with his claim to grant absolution through baptism in the river was a direct challenge to the authority of the temple. No wonder King Herod had him arrested and decapitated. Note that Jesus also claimed the authority to grant absolution and like John before him gave away that absolution freely. He too represented a direct threat to the authority of temple. Thus it was no surprise that he too was executed at the behest of the temple authorities.

Now if the Bible taught that John the Baptist was performing his baptisms for the remission of sins and Christian doctrine held that Jesus was without sin then why did he submit to being baptized? This has long been considered a mystery by the Christian church. The gospels even have John the Baptist demurring from performing the baptism on the grounds that he was not worthy. John only carried out the baptism because Jesus persuaded him that it was necessary.

Why was it necessary if Jesus was without sin? The most common explanation was that Jesus did this simply to be an example to his followers but I never found that a particularly satisfying explanation.

There were rival traditions that were later denounced as heresies and then suppressed. One of these rival traditions held that the baptism of Jesus served the same purpose as the anointing of King Saul and King David, to make Jesus a sacred person and elevate him to the office of messiah. According to this tradition Jesus was not born the Son of God but rather was adopted by God after his baptism. The baptism itself was supposed to serve of purpose of making Jesus fit for that adoption.

I found this a more persuasive explanation. After all, if John's baptisms could elevate a sinful man into a state of divine grace why couldn't the same baptism elevate a man without sin to a son of God?

70) Mockery

While giving her acceptance speech at the Golden Globe Awards, Meryl Streep famously castigated Donald Trump for ridiculing a disabled reporter by mocking his disability. Trump quickly denied the accusation and then proceeded to heap derision upon the actress. Trump's supporters rose to his defense claiming that in fact he was not ridiculing the reporter's disability

No matter how much spin Trump and his followers may give to the incident, one thing is abundantly clear from the video tapes of Trump's speech, he was mocking the reporter and he clearly did so in a manner that was highly suggestive, at least to the casual observer, that the focus of that derision was indeed the reporter's disability.

Now the most interesting thing about this case is the fact that a group of Catholic supporters have chosen to defend Trump by assembling a montage of videos proving that Trump has mocked other people who were not disabled in exactly the same manner. But what does this really prove? It proves that Trump habitually mocks and ridicules those he disagrees with and those who disagree with him. And that he does this so habitually that it has become a normal part of his discourse. He doesn't even see anything wrong with it and, apparently, neither do his supporters.

To my mind Trump's antics during the campaign trail were adequate proof that he was completely unfit to be the President of the United States. The way he mocks people is unbecoming for the leader of the free world. It is undignified and malicious. It displays of smallness of mind and a pettiness which are dangerous qualities for a man with access to nuclear weapons. It is also downright juvenile. I have not personally witnessed such behavior since elementary school. We now have a President with all the maturity of a twelve year old.

I wonder why a man as thin-skinned and intolerant of criticism would seek to occupy the criticism magnet that is the Oval Office. He should have anticipated that he would be criticized mercilessly for his policies alone. Even if he actually possessed the gravitas appropriate for the job. But his childishness simply serves to exacerbate the criticism he was bound to receive anyway. Like anyone who overreacts to teasing he becomes a target for more teasing. People will poke Trump just to see him react. Just like 19th century English gentlemen who used to visit Bedlam to poke the inmates with long sticks.

I can accept Trump's claim that he was not ridiculing Serge Kovaleski's disability, but his behavior is still unacceptable. It is both petty and mean-spirited and we can expect to see much more of it in the months ahead. Most politicians, if they indulge in such behavior at all have sense enough not to do it public. So once again Trump shows that his judgment is every bit as bad as his manners.

71) Defamation

I stated earlier that I regarded Trump's family as off-limits to commentary and criticism. I made that statement under the assumption that the members of Trump's family were simply innocent bystanders to his presidency. I did not feel that they should be subjected to criticism simply because of their familiar relationships with Trump. However, last Monday Melania Trump made herself a legitimate target for criticism.

A lawyer representing Melania Trump filed a defamation suit against the *Daily Mail*. The suit claims that Melania Trump suffered financial hardships resulting from her inability capitalize on unique business opportunities.

What were those unique business opportunities? The suit alleges that an article published by the *Daily Mail* last August prevented Melania from taking full advantage of marketing opportunities presented by the fact that she would become one of the most photographed women in the world for the next several years. The forfeited opportunities included the marketing of a line of products in Melania's name which would have included clothing, accessories, shoes, jewelry, perfume, cosmetics, hair care products and skin care products. Essentially, the lawsuit is claiming $150 million dollars in damages because the *Daily Mail's* article allegedly is preventing Melania Trump from financially exploiting her position as First Lady.

Given the financial hits Ivanka Trump's brand has recently taken, I find it difficult to believe that Melania Trump has much chance of winning this suit. It also creates the distinct impression that Donald Trump's principle motive in running for President was to create business opportunities for himself and his family.

While the lawsuit was clearly filed on Melania's behalf I wonder if she is really the force driving it. I would not be the least bit surprised if Donald Trump wasn't really the instigator of this suit. It just strikes me as an odd thing to do for a First Lady who has remained so much in the background since Trump's inauguration. And it will most likely backfire against the Trumps politically. As if Trump didn't have enough controversy already that he needs to court more.

72) Momentum

Ever since 1992 I have had an on-gain, off-again fascination with the assassination of John F. Kennedy. Over the years I have purchased and read about a hundred books on the subject. The vast majority of those books have argued that the assassination was the product of one conspiracy or another.

I have to admit that I have never found any of the pro-conspiracy arguments particularly compelling. This was largely because those arguments invariably involved emphasizing unreliable evidence in place of reliable evidence and often included the outright distortion of reality.

Conspiracy minded writers tried to prove conspiracy by claiming that the Warren Commission's version of the event was not only highly improbable but completely impossible. An interesting accomplishment if any of them could really carry it out in an honest fashion. Most of them tried to make their own arguments appear more compelling by materially misrepresenting the Warren Commission's case.

These misrepresentations included allegations that the Warren Commission's reconstruction of the assassination proved that one man could not possibly have inflicted all of the wounds on President Kennedy and Governor Connolly.

Writers claimed that the bullet wounds suffered by the two men could not be reconciled with the trajectory of a single bullet. They claimed that for one bullet to have inflicted all of the wounds it would have had to jump up and down and zigzag from right to left. Of course, the writer's own arguments were based on misrepresentations of the relative positioning of the two men with in the limousine during the assassination as well as misrepresentations of the relative positioning of the wounds themselves.

These arguments were popular and were repeated in book after book. But the favorite argument of all involved a misrepresentation of the laws of physics themselves. This argument was the "head-snap" theory.

The "head-snap" theory was an attempt by amateurs with no scientific background to apply the Law of Conservation of Momentum to the assassination. Momentum is a simple enough concept, it is nothing more than mass times velocity. The Law of Conservation of Momentum is an equally simple concept, it holds that the combined momenta of two objects after a collision must equal the combined momenta of the same two objects before the collision.

Writers were quick to note that in physics velocity is a vector quantity. This means that direction is just as important a component to velocity as speed. John Kennedy was sitting motionless in the back of his limousine just before being shot in the head. That means his momentum before the collision was zero.

The fact that he was riding in a moving car can be conveniently ignored as one frame of reference is just as valid as any other. Thus, when analyzing Kennedy's movement before and after the impact of the bullet with his head, one can measure Kennedy's movements relative to the car.

The assassination writers claimed that because of the Law of Conservation of Momentum the direction in which Kennedy falls after being shot in the head must be the same direction that the bullet was traveling just before hitting his head. Since the home movie of the assassination shot by Abraham Zapruder clearly shows Kennedy falling backwards and to the left after the headshot the bullet must have been fired from the right front, the direction of the Grassy Knoll.

The "head-snap" theory was first proposed in Josiah Thompson's *Six Seconds in Dallas* and has been repeated by every conspiracy theorist ever since. Oliver Stone made tremendous use in it in his movie, *JFK*. As I said, it appears to be a very compelling theory and has greatly influenced the general public.

However, the theory relies upon one fundamental assumption, that Kennedy's momentum after the headshot came from the bullet and no other source. The theory fails completely if it can be shown that any momentum was provided by any other source. After all, if any of Kennedy's momentum derived from any source other than the bullet, then no valid conclusions could be drawn about the direction of travel of the bullet based on Kennedy's direction of travel.

Interestingly enough, the assassination researchers who use the "head-snap" theory invariably rely upon empirical observation rather than mathematical analysis when developing their argument. They always fail to acknowledge the fundamental assumption of their theory and therefore fail to prove that a bullet even possesses enough momentum to even produce the head-snap in the first place. Thus the argument is always the same, Kennedy falls backwards and to the left therefore he must have been shot from the right front.

Such an analysis would not even earn a passing grade in the most elementary physics course. I know this because my original major when I attended the University of Maryland was physics. Any analysis of the application of Conservation of Momentum had to include calculations of the momenta of both objects involved in the collision, both before and after the collision. The conspiracy writers have never bothered to do this. Not even the ones supposedly being advised by professional physicists

So, what was John Kennedy's momentum after being shot in the head? It should be a simple enough calculation, mass times velocity. But what is the mass? Do we use John Kennedy's official body weight of 170 pounds? No, for the simple reason that his entire body was not moved by the bullet. However, I suspect that most of it did move at least somewhat. But to favor the conspiracy argument as well as make the calculations simple, I will use only the weight of Kennedy's head. Obviously a great deal more of Kennedy's body mass was involved but it is rather difficult to decided just how much. The average human head weighs ten pounds so that will be the mass I will use in my analysis.

What was Kennedy's velocity when he hit the back seat of his limousine? Only one book attempted to answer this important question, Josiah Thompson's *Six Seconds in Dallas*. Appendix B of that book contained an explanation of how the author's advisor calculated the terminal acceleration at the time Kennedy struck the back seat of the car. As I have nothing wrong with the analysis I readily accepted the figure given. According to the Appendix, Kennedy's terminal acceleration was 94.7 feet per second per second.

One can derive velocity from acceleration simply by multiplying the acceleration by the elapsed time. In this case the time was six frames of a movie with an estimated frame rate of 18 frames per second. That gives the elapsed time as approximately a third of a second. Multiplying acceleration by time yields a velocity of about 32 feet per second. I rounded up to favor the conspiracy argument.

Thus, Kennedy's momentum was his mass of 10 pounds multiplied by his velocity of 32 feet per second to yield a momentum of 320 pounds/feet per second. For the "head-snap" theory to work then the bullet which struck Kennedy in the head had to possess at least 320 pounds/feet per second of momentum.

But how much momentum does a bullet possess? It depends on the weapon used. Bullets come in hundreds of different sizes and powder charges in the cartridges varies a great deal as well. This means the specific combination of mass and velocity varies considerably depending on the weapon and ammunition used. I think we can safely assume that the assassin who shot Kennedy was using a high-powered rifle despite the fact that the House Select

Committee on Assassinations did consider the possibility that a pistol had been used.

Even confining our analysis to just high-powered rifles still leaves hundreds of different combinations of weapon and ammunition to consider. Most military grade ammunition has masses ranging from 100 to 225 grains and exits the barrel at velocities between 2000 and 3000 feet per second.

So, let's consider the most powerful version. An Armor Piercing M1930 round weighing 184 grains and traveling at 2790 feet per second.

I chose this bullet as the most power rifle bullet listed in my source material. The cartridges with the largest bullets tended to have the smallest powder charges and thus the lowest muzzle velocities while the cartridges with the highest muzzle velocities tended to also have the smallest bullets.

The mass and velocity of the M1930 round yields a momentum of 513,360 grain/feet per second. Sounds impressive, doesn't it? Yet we have that slight problem that our momenta do not use the same units of measurement. We'll have to correct that deficiency if our analysis is going to be meaningful.

Bullets travel very fast but they don't weigh much. That is why their weights are measured in grains rather than ounces. How many grains are in a pound? 5000. So to convert the bullet's momentum to match the units used in calculating Kennedy's momentum we will have to divide that 513,360 grains/feet per second by 5000 to convert it into pounds/feet per second. The result is 103 pounds/feet per second. As you can see, that is nowhere near the 320 pounds/feet per second required to account for Kennedy's movement after being shot in the head.

The explanation for the discrepancy is simple enough. Physicist Luiz Alvarez gave it years ago. The backward and leftward motion seen in Kennedy after being shot in the head was not caused by the impact of the bullet, rather it was caused by the explosion of blood and brain tissue out of the side of Kennedy's head which occurred immediately after the transiting of the fatal bullet. The blood and tissue exploded towards the right front, driving Kennedy's head and body towards the left rear. This is clearly shown in the Zapruder film but it goes by so quickly it is not noticeable unless you view the film frame by frame.

Now the assassination writers all claim to have studied the Zapruder film frame by frame. Some even claimed to have seen the movie at normal speed. Yet none of them seemed to have noticed the eruption of blood and brain tissue immediately after the head shot. But the fact is that all of them noticed it. It's just that none of them appreciated its true significance. This is the sort of thing that happens when laymen with no scientific background try to apply the laws of physics to a complex, real-world situation.

73) Highway Robbery

Civil asset forfeiture laws allow local law enforcement agencies to confiscate the property of suspected criminals. Property seized in this way is often divided between the seizing agency and the local prosecutor's office. When properly used such laws can be a valuable tool in law enforcement. When abused those same laws can become a form of legalized highway robbery.

For years stories of the abuse of civil asset forfeiture have appeared in the mainstream media. Texas seems particularly prone to this abuse but it has occurred in many other states as well. There have been reports of thousands of dollars worth of cash and assets seized for even minor traffic infractions.

In 2007 Jennifer Boatright and Ron Henderson were pulled over in Tenaha, Texas for driving more than half a mile in the left lane without passing. Once stopped, the officer searched their car and found a marble pipe and $6,037 in cash. The officer brought Boatright and Henderson to the police station. There the district attorney threatened to charge them criminally if they did not agree to allow the police to confiscate their cash. Texas law allows the police to seize assets without even charging the owners of those assets with a crime, the mere suspicion of criminal activity is sufficient.

Two Texas State Senators, Republican Konni Burton and Democrat Juan Hinojosa have proposed legislation that would require a criminal conviction before civil asset forfeiture could be imposed. Obviously this proposed legislation is meant to end the abuses of jurisdictions like Tenaha with a long and well documented history of abuse.

Who would oppose such common-sense legal reform? Why, certain Texas sheriffs and Donald Trump. Trump recently hosted a meeting at the White House with county sheriffs from around the country, including Texas. One of those sheriffs, Harold Eavenson of Rockwall County, Texas complained about the proposed legislation. Trump jokingly said that he would destroy the careers of the two senators and invited Sheriff Eavenson to name them.

I suspect that no one bothered to inform Trump of the pattern of abuse of civil asset forfeiture which allowed certain unscrupulous law enforcement agencies and prosecutor's offices to legally steal from innocent travelers. I suspect that the only thing Trump was told was that such legal reform would benefit drug traffickers and Trump, in true knee-jerk fashion, immediately pontificated on how anybody in the Texas legislature could possibly side with drug dealers over law enforcement.

74) Betsy DeVos

The confirmation of Betsy DeVos as Secretary of Education was the triumph of partisan politics over the national interest. In confirming DeVos the Senate abdicated its constitutionally mandated duty to ensure that the people whom the President appoints are qualified for the offices they are meant to hold.

DeVos is completely and utterly lacking in even the most rudimentary qualifications. In fact, the only apparent reason for her nomination in the first place was her status as a major contributor to the Republican Party. Senate Republicans with only two exceptions voted to confirm DeVos. The vote was 50-50 with Vice President Pence casting the tie-breaking vote to confirm her.

The fact that almost all of the senators voted along party lines seems particularly disturbing to me. Is it really possible that fifty Republican senators all thought that DeVos is qualified to be Secretary of Education? I strongly suspect that this vote reflects party discipline more than party consensus. It's as if the Republicans in the Senate are rubber stamping Trump's appointments no matter how inappropriate they might be.

It seems to me that the appointment of a rank amateur to head the Department of Education is a slap in the face to all professional educators. It seems like a fundamental denial of the validity of the education profession. In appointing DeVos Trump is essentially saying that no special qualifications are needed for formulating and implementing education policies.

I have no idea what will happen over the next four years, but I suspect that the press will take a greater interest in the Education Department than it has taken in the past.

75) The Girl King

Last August I saw *The Girl King*. It was a decent movie but there really wasn't anything exceptional about it. The movie was about Queen Christina who was Queen of Sweden from her father's death in battle in 1632 until her abdication in 1654. As Christina was only six years old at the time of her ascension, the country was ruled by a regent until 1644.

The Girl King portrays Christina as a lesbian. This judgment was based upon her penchant for wearing men's clothing coupled with the fact that she never married. While she may well have been a lesbian, the historical record is not completely unambiguous on this point.

The movie sought to represent that Christina's abdication was prompted by her sexuality. This was accomplished by focusing so much on her sexuality and her personal life while focusing so little on the character of her reign. In this way the writer and director were able to conveniently ignore the profligacy with which Christina administered her kingdom. Had Christina been a more capable ruler it is highly doubtful that her sexuality would have been an issue at all. The sexuality of capable rulers never seems to have been a serious issue. Elizabeth I of England, for example, never married either, but she was not forced to abdicate over her unwillingness to produce an heir and there were no rumors alleging lesbianism.

The movie not only largely ignored the internal politics of mid-sixteenth century Sweden in favor of focusing on Christina's love life, it also largely ignored the external politics of the time.

At the beginning of Christina's reign Sweden was still embroiled in the Thirty Years War. That war, which was the bloodiest war in European history up to that time, began as a struggle between Catholics and Protestants over the souls of the German people and ended as a struggle between the Hapsburgs and the Bourbons over political power.

Christina very much wanted to end the war while her Chancellor wanted the war to continue. Christina had her way and the war ended with the Peace of Westphalia. This treaty established the Balance of Power as the basis of European diplomacy. The Peace of Westphalia also established the principle of political sovereignty. The signatories recognized that each state had the right to determine its own domestic policies without interference from other states. This in turn established the principle, at least in theory, that the sovereign would determine the religion of the state. In practice, however, it worked the other way around. Instead of the sovereign determining the religion of the people it was the people who determined the religion of the sovereign.

As case in point, when King James II of England began to openly practice Catholicism his Protestant subjects found him unfit to rule and after just three years parliamentary leaders offered the English throne to the Protestant Prince William III of Orange.

Despite the attempts of *The Girl King* to portray Christina's abdication as being caused by her sexuality, the real reasons were her fiscal irresponsibility and her conversion to Catholicism. Protestant Sweden would no more tolerate a Catholic sovereign than Protestant England or Protestant Scotland. This was a movie where sexual politics definitely took precedence over historical reality .

76) Copywriting

Copywriting is one of the inevitable tasks which comes with publishing a book. Copywriting is the creation of advertising and promotional material to accompany the book. It can be as simple as choosing the keywords and writing a description of the book for online vendors. But it can also include composing the back cover description and other advertising materials in the event you choose to advertise the book through Facebook or Amazon.

Naturally, one can hire the services of a professional copywriter. I'm not sure what the price for that would be but I am sure the service is much more economical than editing services tend to be. Unfortunately, I've never had the wherewithal to hire a professional copywriter, so I've always had to perform those duties myself.

I don't find copywriting to be particularly burdensome. Whenever I've put my mind to the task I've always found that the appropriate words came to mind readily enough. I did try my hand at running advertisements for some of my books near the beginning of last year.

First I tried with Facebook, but they never ran my ad. Rather, they promptly flagged my account for "suspicious activity" and refused to run it. Within two hours of my account being flagged I submitted proof of my identity to Facebook. When they failed to take any action at all after ten days I withdrew my request for assistance and simply didn't bother to use their advertising services again.

Next, I ran an advertisement on Amazon. I had no trouble with them and my ads ran as planned. I even increased my sales ever so slightly, though not enough for the increased royalties to pay for the advertising. After this experience I decided not to run any more ads. At least not for the books which I have already published.

I might try my hand at advertising again, if *Thoughts Out of Season* shows any signs of marketing promise. Who knows, if I finally experience some modicum of success with my publishing efforts I might even be in the market for a professional editor. One can always dream.

77) Compartmentalization

My life has always been rather highly compartmentalized. This hasn't been the result of some well thought out plan. I suppose it was just a natural development for me.

My life can be divided into discreet phases with the beginning and end of each phase marked by determining events in my life. Such events include jobs I have held and schools I have attended. Some periods of my life were even defined by my online activities.

There were times when I participated in news groups. Times when I participated in online auctions. There were even times when I participated in online stock trading. I thought those were activities which I would engage in forever, especially the stock trading. But all of them proved to be nothing more than passing fads.

Generally speaking, the relationships I entered into during a particular phase in my life did not carry over into the next phase. This was why the longest friendship I ever had in my life lasted nine years. Other people might have lifelong friends but that has never been my experience. Again, this was not planned. And these relationships helped to define the particular compartment of my life.

Phases of my life usually lasted for a number of years. This was due to a fundamental conservatism about my life. I usually didn't change anything until change was forced upon me. I have always been a creature of habit. There have been exceptions, however. My participation in a newsgroup dedicated to discussion of the Kennedy Assassination ended because I grew tired of the adversarial attitudes of so many of the participants. I see that same adversarial attitude dominating politics today.

Sometimes friendships ended because they were too high maintenance. If a friendship requires a lot of effort on my part to maintain and I sense that this effort was not being reciprocated I would simply stop making the effort. Naturally, the friendship then died a natural death.

Some friendships were born out of common interest. In those cases the friendships would last as long as we both participated in that common interest. But, like many other aspects of life, interests change. When that happened the bond between us broke and we drifted apart in the sea of life.

I have never consciously ended a friendship or any other relationship. Most of the time I didn't even notice the exact moment when the relationship ended. I simply lost contact with the person and this lack of contact caused the emotional bond to wither and die. It might be months or even years later before I realized what had happened.

Interestingly enough the one exception to this overall pattern has been my relationship with my ex-wife. We are still friends even years after our divorce. I have known her for eight years now and every sign points towards our relationship growing stronger rather than weaker. The divorce was caused by a fundamental change in our relationship from romantic to platonic. Oddly enough this change in the nature of our relationship caused it to grow stronger rather than weaker.

78) Economics

The United States has long prided itself on having the highest standard of living in the world and for many decades this has been true. However, with a higher standard of living comes a greater cost of living. The reason why America was able to sustain its high standard of living was because American income was also the highest in the world. In fact, the high American standard of living was a direct result of the income effect. Americans had the highest standard of living because they also enjoyed the highest level of income. The two were interrelated.

The rise of American income and with it the American standard of living was driven by the rise of industrialization in America. The growth of manufacturing greatly reduced the cost of producing consumer goods. This lowering of cost produced a favorable income effect as people could afford to buy more consumer goods.

Manufacturing was both highly efficient and greatly profitable. It was also both very labor and capital intensive. The rise in manufacturing led to the rise in demand for both capital goods and labor. This increase in the demand for labor caused a rise the price manufacturers were willing to pay for labor. As manufacturing wages rose, labor shifted from agriculture to manufacturing which in turn caused the mechanization of agriculture. This mechanization needed more manufacturing to support it. The rise of manufacturing also became self sustaining as more manufacturing was needed to produce the machinery used by the factories.

It was not just the demands of the labor market that caused the rise of the wages of factory workers. The rise of the labor union movement played an even bigger role. It was the collective bargaining of unionized manufacturing workers that really made factory jobs among the highest paying in the country.

In a very real sense America is a victim of its own success. As I said before the highest standard of living in the world comes with it the highest cost of living. Because the cost of living was lower in most of the rest of the world, workers in countries like China and Mexico can afford to work for less than an American worker could live from.

This was what has been driving the outsourcing phenomenon in American manufacturing. While taxes and regulations clearly also played a role, the primary reason for the competitive advantage enjoyed by foreign workers over American workers was the lower cost of labor.

Because of this it was simply not possible to buy American without paying more. The outsourcing phenomenon would never have developed this far if there hadn't been constant economic pressure from the American public on retailers and by extension on manufacturers to lower costs. When given the choice between buying cheaper goods made in China or Mexico and buying more expensive goods made in America, the American public has consistently bought foreign made goods. That was the reason why so many consumer goods are now manufactured in China.

Trump has promised to bring manufacturing jobs back to America and reverse decades of outsourcing. I do not see how he could possibly accomplish this without greatly increasing the cost of consumer goods. The economics are just not on Trump's side.

79) The Calendar

Our reckoning of time has always been based on astronomical observations. Our days our based on the apparent revolution of the sun around the earth caused by the earth's rotation. Our months are based upon the lunar cycle. Our year is based upon the discovery by Egyptian astrologers that the star Sirius rises with the sun once every 365 days.

As time passed and our astronomical observations became more accurate, we have updated our calendars to reflect these new observations. In the first century B.C. the Greek astronomer, Sosigenes, discovered that the year was

365.25 days long rather than 365 days. Julius Caesar duly corrected the calendar by instituting the custom of the leap year, adding an extra day to every fourth year.

In the 16th century astronomers further refined the length of the year. The new measurement set the length of the year at 365.242 days. Pope Gregory XIII duly edited the calendar to reflect this refinement. Where the Julian calendar incorporated 25 leap years in each century, the Gregorian calendar has only 24 leap years in each century except in centuries that are evenly divisible by 500. This meant that years ending in 00 are not leap years unless the year is evenly divisible by 500. Thus the year 2000 was leap year while 1900 was not.

The names of our days were derived from the ancient Roman calendar. The Romans named the days of the week in honor of the heavenly bodies with the order of precedence determined roughly by brightness. Thus the names were *Dies Solis*, "Day of the Sun", *Dies Lunae*, "Day of the Moon", *Dies Martis*, "Mars' Day", *Dies Mercurii*, Mercury's Day, *Dies Jovis*, Jupiter's Day, *Dies Veneris*, Venus' Day, and *Dies Saturni*, Saturn's Day.

At some point after the fall of the Western Roman Empire the names of the Roman gods in the days of the week were replaced with the names of their Anglo-Saxon equivalents. Thus, *Dies Solis* became Sunday, *Dies Lunae* became Moonday or Monday, *Dies Martis* became Tuesday, *Dies Mercurii* became Wodensday or Wednesday, *Dies Jovis* became Thursday while *Dies Veneris* became Freyasday or Friday. As Saturn had no Nordic equivalent, *Dies Saturni* simply became anglicized to Saturday.

It is interesting to note that Jupiter was equated with Thor and Mercury with Odin despite the fact that Odin was revered as the king of the Norse gods. Thor was a caster of lightning which was also the most obvious attribute of Jupiter. Most likely Odin's equation with Mercury was due to the fact that Odin gathered the souls of fallen heroes and carried them to Valhalla, or rather his handmaidens, the Valkyries, did this for him.

The names of our months also came from the ancient Roman calendar. January was named after Janus, the Roman god of beginnings.

February was named after Februalia, a purification festival important in ancient Roman culture.

March was named in honor of the God, Mars, and was originally the first month of the Roman year.

The origin of the name April is unknown. The ancient Romans themselves believed that it was derived from aperire, meaning "to open." The traditional explanation for the name of the month was that April was the month when fruits and flowers opened.

May was named for Maia, a Roman Goddess who likely personified the growth of cereal crops. The name seems to have signified "growing great."

June, July and August were named for mortal men, though two of those men were later deified. June was named for Junius Brutus, the founder of the Roman Republic. July was named in honor of Julius Caesar and August was named for Augustus Caesar.

September, October, November and December were not originally names at all but numbers. They literally meant "Month Number Seven", "Month Number Eight", "Month Number Nine" and "Month Number Ten" respectively.

June was named so long ago that the month's original name has since been lost in time. July was original called Quinctilis, "Month Number Five", while August was named Sextilis, "Month Number Six."

These names reflected three facts about the ancient Roman calendar. The first fact, as I mentioned before, was that March was originally the first month of the year. The second fact was that the Roman calendar originally contained only ten months. The months of January and

February were added later. And the third was the fact that the ancient Romans were often terribly unimaginative when it came to naming conventions.

This lack of imagination was also reflected in their personal names. The ancient Romans only commonly used 21 personal names. Of the three elements typically seen in an ancient Roman name, called by them the Praenomen, the Nomen and the Cognomen, only the Praenomen or first name was the personal name. The nomen or middle name was the family name or surname and the most important component. The cognomen or last name was the branch of the family to which the owner of the name belonged. Thus, for Gaius Julius Caesar, Gaius was his Praenomen or personal name. Julius was his Nomen or the name of his family and Caesar was his Cognomen or the branch of the Julius family to which he belonged.

The usual naming convention was for the eldest son to bear the same name as the father, though some Roman families did follow the Greek tradition of naming the eldest son after the grandfather. The younger sons would receive a different Praenomen. This tradition was followed for generations. So, for many of the oldest and most prominent families we see the same names appearing over and over and over again in Roman history.

The situation was even worse for women. The ancient Romans did not give their daughters Praenomens. A daughter was simply given the feminized version of the father's nomen. Thus, many names that have now become personal names such as Julia and Claudia were originally the feminine form of ancient Roman family names. What happened if a Roman father had more than one daughter? They would all receive the same name but would be differentiated by the addition of "Prima" and "Secunda" to the name. This essentially meant that they were called "Daughter Number One" and "Daughter Number Two."

80) Proportional Voting

Earlier I proposed replacing the winner take all scheme for allocation electoral votes with a scheme which would allocate the electoral votes among the candidates in proportion to the popular votes which they earned in that same state. The way this would work would be that if the Republican candidate won 60% of a state's popular vote while the Democratic candidate won 40% of the vote then the Republican candidate would receive 60% of the state's electoral votes while the Democratic candidate would win 40%. I think this would be a fairer and more democratic way of allocating the states' electoral votes as the electoral vote would more closely follow the popular vote.

As an experiment I re-examined the 2016 Presidential Election, allocating the states' electoral votes proportionately instead of using the winner take all system. My method was simple enough. I examined the election returns from each state on a case by case basis. I took the total number of electoral votes for each state and multiplied it by the percentage of the popular vote which each candidate received. The result was the number of electoral votes which each candidate would have received had the electoral votes by allocated proportionally. In cases where the total votes allocated was less than the total number which the state possessed, I assigned the unallocated votes to the candidate with the highest popular vote total.

During the actual election the winner take all method was utilized by most states. The result was that Donald Trump won 304 electoral votes to Hilary Clinton's 227. This was despite the fact that Hilary Clinton had actually won the popular vote. When I reallocated the electoral votes according to my own proportional scheme, Hilary Clinton won 272 electoral votes to Donald Trump's 266. Had my system been used Hilary Clinton would be

President of the United States today rather than Donald Trump.

The actual allocation of electoral votes worked out as follows:

Name of State	Electoral Votes	% Of Popular Vote Clinton	% Of Popular Vote Trump	Allocated Electoral Votes Clinton	Allocated Electoral Votes Trump
Alabama	9	34.40%	62.18%	3	6
Alaska	3	36.55%	51.28%	1	2
Arizona	11	45.4%	49.0%	5	6
Arkansas	6	33.7%	60.6%	2	4
California	55	61.73%	31.62%	38	17
Colorado	9	48.1%	43.3%	5	4
Connecticut	7	54.57%	40.93%	4	3
Delaware	3	53.4%	41.9%	2	1
District of Columbia	3	90.5%	4.1%	3	0
Florida	29	47.85	49.2%	14	15
Georgia	16	45.9%	51.1%	7	9
Hawaii	4	62.2%	30.0%	3	1
Idaho	4	27.5%	59.2%	1	3
Illinois	20	55.83%	38.76%	12	8
Indiana	11	37.8%	56.9%	4	7
Iowa	6	41.7%	51.2%	3	3
Kansas	6	36.0%	56.6%	2	4
Kentucky	8	32.7%	62.5%	3	5
Louisiana	8	38.4%	58.1%	3	5
Maine	4	47.8%	44.9%	2	2
Maryland	10	60.34%	32.92%	7	3
Massachusetts	11	60.0%	32.8%	7	4
Michigan	16	47.27%	47.5%	8	8
Minnesota	10	46.44%	44.92%	6	4
Mississippi	6	40.1%	57.9%	2	4
Missouri	10	38.1%	56.8%	4	6
Montana	3	33.2%	56.6%	1	2

Nebraska	5	33.7%	58.7%	2	3
Nevada	6	47.92%	45.5%	3	3
New Hampshire	4	47.8%	47.5%	2	2
New Jersey	14	55.45%	41.35%	8	6
New Mexico	5	48.2%	40.0%	3	2
New York	29	59.0%	36.52%	18	11
North Carolina	15	46.17%	49.83%	7	8
North Dakota	3	27.2%	63.0%	1	2
Ohio	18	43.56%	51.69%	8	10
Oklahoma	7	28.9%	65.3%	2	5
Oregon	7	50.07%	39.09%	4	3
Pennsylvania	20	47.85%	48.56%	10	10
Rhode Island	4	54.4%	39.0%	2	2
South Carolina	9	40.7%	54.9%	4	5
South Dakota	3	31.7%	61.5%	1	2
Tennessee	11	34.7%	60.7%	4	7
Texas	38	43.24%	52.23%	16	22
Utah	6	27.46%	45.54%	2	4
Vermont	3	55.7%	30.3%	2	1
Virginia	13	49.7%	44.4%	7	6
Washington	12	54.3%	38.07%	7	5
West Virginia	5	26.5%	68.6%	1	4
Wisconsin	10	46.45%	47.22%	5	5
Wyoming	3	21.9%	68.2%	1	2
Total	538	48.0%	45.9%	272	266

Naturally, the Republicans, especially Trump supporters would oppose any changes to the electoral laws. "If it isn't broke don't fix it" would be their attitude. Of course, they would take the opposite point of view if the results had gone the other way. If Hilary Clinton had lost the popular vote but won the electoral vote. Ultimately, my system is not meant to favor one party over the other but rather to eliminate the problem of candidates winning the electoral vote while losing the popular vote.

81) A Business Decision

Donald Trump has recently complained on Twitter that Nordstrom's acted unfairly when it dropped Ivanka Trump's clothing and accessories lines from its website and its stores. Nordstrom's said that it was a business decision based upon the poor market performance of those lines. I would expect that Trump of all people would understand the nature of business and the mercilessness of the market. Why he would expect business decisions to be fair is completely beyond me.

Now having said that, there is an organized boycott of all of Trump's brands including the brands of his daughter. Naturally, this boycott is politically motivated. It is a protest against Trump's administration and his policies. But even if the boycott is the proximal cause of Nordstrom's decision, it is still at heart a business decision.

In fact, the only way that I can see that this decision would be unfair would be if it had been a political decision rather than a business decision. That would have been the case if Nordstrom's decision had not been based on marketing performance but as a reaction to Trump's political policies or if the decision had been directed at Ivanka Trump personally. If Nordstrom had removed her lines simply because she is the daughter of the President.

But fair or not, Nordstrom's certainly has the right to decide which products it will sell and which ones it will not. Is it fair for Trump to use his position as President of the United States to seek to promote the business interests of his children?

Trump's supporters might claim that he is acting as a private citizen rather than as President of the United States, but such arguments are specious. Trump is President twenty-four hours a day, seven days a week. He simply cannot separate himself from his office and everything he says or does reflects upon that office.

82) The Biggest Mistake

I think Donald Trump's decision to run for President of the United States is proving to be the biggest mistake he ever made in his life. As President Trump has been subjected to a degree of scrutiny that he would never have experienced as a private citizen. His every word and deed is being recorded and analyzed. The eyes of the world are upon him and most of those eyes are far from friendly.

Now the whole world will witness whether or not he can actually live up to his own hype. If in the end he proves to be an incompetent dupe or if he is forced out of office in disgrace, his personal brand might never recover from the damage.

I wonder about his refusal to release his tax returns as all of his predecessors have done. His critics believe that this refusal was due to his business dealings creating conflicts of interest with his duties as President. But I wonder if there might be another reason entirely for this refusal. Perhaps Trump isn't as rich as he claims. That might negatively impact his businesses more than a potential conflict of interest could.

83) The Ultimate Capitalists

The Soviet Union proclaimed itself the fulfillment of Karl Marx's prophecy that the proletariat would rise up against the capitalist bourgeoisie and replace it with a communist society. Marx himself identified the capitalists as a small minority of wealthy men whose wealth allowed them to monopolize all of the means of production. Through their control over the means of production they were able to reduce the proletariat to the status of slaves. Furthermore, Marx believed that the capitalists were able to maintain their system through their control over the government which then came to serve the interests of the bourgeoisie.

With communism Marx foresaw a society where the proletariat would own and control the means of production instead of wealthy capitalist exploiters. In fact, Marx believed that the proletariat would institute their communist society only after a violent revolution during which the capitalists would be swept away. After all, if the capitalists controlled the government and the government served the interests of the capitalists, then violent revolution was the only way of changing the situation.

The Soviet Union claimed that the Bolshevik Revolution of 1917 was the fulfillment of this prophecy. The Bolsheviks themselves claimed to be a cadre of revolutionaries who would lead the proletariat in establishing the communist society which Marx had foreseen.

What happened in reality was that the Bolsheviks gained control of the government and made themselves the only legal party in Russia. With firm control over the government the Bolsheviks seized control of the means of production through the expedient of nationalizing all business concerns and private property. The government owned everything and the newly renamed Communist Party of the Soviet Union controlled the government.

Never in its 74 years of existence did either Communist Russia or its successor state, The Union of Soviet Socialist Republics, ever turn the means of production over to the proletariat as they promised. Never did they even begin the process of preparing the proletariat for control over the means of production as they promised.

In fact, the Soviet Union was ever only communist in name. Had Marx himself ever witnessed it, he would have immediately recognized it for what it truly was, the ultimate capitalistic state.

Remember that Marx did not define capitalism in terms of the private ownership of the means of production but in the control over the means of production by a small group. True communism was not state ownership of the means of production, it was collective ownership of the means of production. The Soviet Union was the ultimate capitalist state because the proletariat never collectively owned or controlled the means of production. The means of production was always owned by the state and controlled by the party. Thus, instead of being the cadre of the proletariat, the Communist Party of the Soviet Union was in reality a society of capitalists.

With their complete control over the government and the government's complete ownership of everything, the Communist Party of the Soviet Union was able to exploit the Russian workers more thoroughly and more mercilessly than any capitalist bourgeoisie could ever manage. Far from being true communists they were truly the ultimate capitalists.

George Orwell understood this. That is why he ended *Animal Farm* the way he did. In *Animal Farm* the humans represented the capitalists, the farm animals represented the proletariat and the pigs represented the Communist Party. At the end of the novel the pigs became indistinguishable to the other animals from the humans. Orwell saw the Soviet Union not as the fulfillment of Marx but as the antithesis of true Marxism.

84) Obsession and Compulsion

As February slowly passes by and I find myself drawing inexorably closer and closer to the completion of this manuscript, I find myself becoming increasingly obsessed with completing it and compelled to finish it. I don't really know how healthy this truly is but it has allowed me to increase my productivity immensely. Here I am only halfway through the week and already I have written more material this week than I have for a one week period in any of the previous five weeks.

Right at this moment I have already written 3,790 words today and 13,119 words for the week. For a comparison my productivity during the first week was 4,882 words. During the second week it was 2,309 words. I wrote 4,493 words the third week, 10,048 words the fourth week and 8,147 words the fifth week.

If I can maintain this level of production I will finish the manuscript before the end of this week. Then I will have the task of editing it before I can submit it for publication.

I have already begun considering the back cover copy. I intend to write a disclaimer warning Trump supporters that the contents of the book will be likely to upset them. Something along the lines of "Warning: This book contains material highly critical of Donald Trump, his administration and his policies. Reader discretion is advised." I suspect that this just might help stir the pot just a little bit.

85) A Warning

Seth Klarman is a hedge fund manager whose fund has been profitable for 31 of the last 34 years. The performance of his fund has given him a reputation for expertise in market analysis and made his advice highly sought after. Recently he sent his clients a newsletter in which he criticized Donald Trump's policies.

Despite the recent upsurge in the markets after Trump's election, Mr. Klarman warns that Trump's policies are likely to undermine the markets in the long run.

Mr. Klarman believes that Trump's protectionist policies cannot work in the long run. They are irresponsible and will simply bolster market inefficiency. This in turn will lead to inflation and rising interest rates. The tax cuts which Trump intends to implement will balloon the deficit and further swell the national debt to the point where it will negatively impact the economy in the future.

Mr. Klarman also believes that Trump's overconfidence is more indicative of poor judgment than of strong leadership. This coupled with Trump's proven record for volatility will further exacerbate America's economic problems. On the whole, Mr. Klarman believes that Trump is not fit for the Oval Office. He even wrote before the election that it was "simply unthinkable that Donald Trump could become our president." It should be noted that Mr. Klarman is not a liberal Democrat but a pragmatic independent who often donates to political candidates from both parties.

86) 46%

Only 46% of the electorate actually voted for Donald Trump in the last presidential election. Yet even that rather unimpressive statistic most likely exaggerated his political support on the day of his election. Many of those who voted for Trump, perhaps even most, weren't really voting *for* Trump as much as they were voting *against* Hilary Clinton.

Had the Democrats come up with a more broadly appealing candidate Donald Trump would not have won the election at all. Clinton was widely perceived by the voters as too liberal and too establishmentarian. How much damage Clinton's campaign took from the hacking of democratic servers perpetrated by the Russians we will never know.

I believe that a lot of Trump's support came from his presentation of himself as a maverick who would overturn the status quo. He sought to tap into popular discontent with the vested interests who seem to have too much influence over Washington. His promise to "drain the swamp" resonated with some voters and explains why he enjoyed so much support in the Midwest, the West and the South.

However, I believe that Trump will ultimately prove to be a disappointment. His cabinet choices seem to indicate that the election of Trump to the Oval Office has merely replaced one set of special interest groups for another. The "swamp" is not going to be drained, there will simply be a substitution of one set of alligators for another.

We all know that Trump has his supporters. They are quite vocal on the internet and social media. But how many of them are there, really? The attendance at the inauguration certainly suggests that Trump's support even then was quite a bit smaller than even his rather unimpressive election returns seem to suggest.

Right now opinion polls show that Trump's approval ratings are the lowest in history. Considering how short his tenure in office has been that is a sign that his term of office is not going to be much fun for the thin skinned chief executive. He will have to perform quite a coup to reverse that decidedly negative trend.

87) Trump and Hitler

Some people, especially on social media, have made comparisons between Donald Trump and Adolf Hitler. These people draw supposed parallels between the President and the German dictator in order to denigrate Trump. I find such comparisons inappropriate examples of political hyperbole. Comparing Trump to Hitler is like comparing a school yard bully to Pablo Escobar.

The evidence for Trump's racism, his stereotypical comments about Mexican immigrants and his comments on the Mexican heritage of a judge he disliked, paled in comparison to the anti-Semitism and homophobia practiced and preached by Hitler. Trump has not advocated denying civil rights to Hispanics or Muslims. He has not built concentration camps across the country to mass detain Muslims and Hispanics.

While trump did indeed invoke fear during his campaign for President and continues to do so as President he has never taken it to the heights taken by Hitler during his political career.

While Trump has more than once openly espoused imperialism, once during his speech at CIA headquarters and again during a more recent interview, he has not advocated world conquest as the means of solving America's economic problems or to pay for his programs.

While Trump has promised to bring jobs back to American workers just as Hitler promised to bring jobs to German workers, it is unlikely that Trump will be able to fulfill this promise. This was a promise that Hitler kept, but at the price of militarizing Germany and then launching World War II.

Trump does not exercise the control over the news media in America that Hitler had exercised over the news media in Germany. Here the news media does not need permission from Sean Spicer to publish or broadcast. The news media in Germany needed a license from Goebbels and that license could be revoked at any time. I suspect though that Trump perhaps wishes he could control the news media in the same way.

Trump does not have the charisma that Hitler had. The German dictator was legendary for his ability to mesmerize crowds and hold them in the palm of his hand. If Trump had that sort of oratorical prowess he would be dangerous indeed. He also would not have so much opposition or suffer the denigration he has had to endure. While Hitler was chancellor of Germany he was widely regarded, even outside of Germany, as a political genius.

Trump has not raised his own personal army the way Hitler did with his Sturm Abteilungen and his SS. Trump has not indulged in the extra-judicial killings which Hitler authorized at the beginning of his rule and were a hallmark of his reign.

While Trump's slogans such as "Make America Great Again" and "America First" do have a Hitlerian flavor to them I don't read too much into that. Trump's management style also bears a slight cosmetic resemblance to Hitler's. Trump certainly has a taste for autocracy. He sometimes indulges in the same type of brow-beating and bullying which Hitler would employ at times, especially in closed door meetings with foreign leaders.

But Hitler had more of a flair for the dramatic. And Hitler did a much better job at selling false narratives to justify his actions. When Hitler wanted an excuse to suppress his political opponents, he staged a fire at the Reichstag. When Hitler wanted to invade Poland he made it look like Poland had invaded Germany. If Trump were as adept at this type of treachery there would be no opposition to his policies.

My own opposition to Trump is not based on any supposed similarity between him and Hitler. Rather it is based upon the stupidity of some of his policies and the incompetent way that his administration is going to carry out those policies. Trump is not nearly the politician Hitler was and I think we can all be thankful for that.

88) The Nature of Evil

What was evil? Webster's Ninth New College Dictionary defined evil as "something that brings sorrow, distress or calamity." Thus, evil could be anything that caused harm either to the individual or to society as a whole. Not surprisingly, philosophers and theologians have wrestled with the nature and origin of evil for thousands of years. In fact, the nature of evil was one of the central foci of both religion and moral philosophy.

Evil can come in one of two main forms. Human evil, harm caused by individuals or groups and natural evil, harm caused by natural phenomena.

Human evil seemed easy enough to explain at first. To the ancient Jews it was simply the product of free will. All people had the choice between whether to obey God's will or disobey it. Good was obedience to God's will while evil was disobedience to God's will.

Natural evil was a little trickier. For the most part nature was benevolent. Human life would be impossible if this was not the case. But there were times when the forces of nature caused harm. The same sun that caused the crops to ripen could also make them wither. The rains that brought life giving water could also bring devastating floods. The same winds that brought cool breezes and trade winds brought destructive storms. Sometimes the very earth shook under men's feet. Then there was the mystery of disease. There was a central ambivalence to the forces of nature that man found profoundly disturbing.

In ancient times men conceived of the forces of nature as personified by gods. As the forces of nature were for the most part benevolent, so were the gods that represented them. But as the forces of nature could also be destructive from time to time so could the gods. Men came to conceive of the gods as ultra powerful humans. Thus men imbued these gods with personalities patterned after the personalities of men. Because of the development of this concept, nature's destructiveness came to be understood as the physical manifestation of divine wrath.

As the anger of men could be assuaged by flattery and the giving of gifts, it stood to reason that the anger of the gods could likewise to assuaged by the same methods. This was the theory that drove the development of religion. Worship was a form of flattery and sacrifice was a form of gift giving. Through religion ancient man hoped to avoid or at least minimize the occurrence of natural evil.

In some ways the development of monotheism among the ancient Jews was revolutionary. While every other culture conceived of the world as full of gods of greater or lesser power, each of whom was the personification of some aspect of the natural world, the ancient Jews came to believe that there was really only one god that controlled all of the forces of nature. But in other ways Jewish monotheism was little different from gentile polytheism. Like the gentiles, the Jews continued to believe that natural evil was a result of divine wrath. There was one rather minor but important difference, however.

While the wrath of the gentile gods was often provoked by neglect or wounded pride, the wrath of the Jewish god was provoked by human disobedience to divine will. The gentile gods didn't demand good behavior from their worshippers, just worship and sacrifice while the prophets of the Jewish god proclaimed that God delighted in obedience to his will not in sacrifice. Thus the gentiles believed that human evil was the result of personal wickedness but natural evil was the result of the temperaments and mercurial dispositions of the gods. The Jews saw the root of all evil, both human and natural, in human disobedience to God's will. They believed that the world would have been a paradise but for the disobedience of the first men, Adam and Eve.

The sixth century B.C. brought another fundamental change to theological thought. Zarathustra, more commonly known as Zoroaster, explained the existence of good and evil in the world in terms of the conflict between the forces of light and the forces of darkness. In Zarathustra's teachings, which are now known as Zoroastrianism, Ahura Mazda personified the forces of light while Angra Mainyu personified the forces of darkness. All good came from Ahura Mazda and all evil came from Angra Mainyu. This was true both of natural evil and of human evil as human evil was believed to be the product of Angra Mainyu's malign influence on the human psyche.

Zarathustra's thinking came to influence every major religion in the region, including Judaism. Whereas before all evil was simply the consequence of free will now the Jews came to believe that evil was caused by the influence of an evil supernatural being.

By the time Zarathustra's moral philosophy began to influence Jewish thought, the Jew's monotheism was far too ingrained in their thinking for them to accept the existence of another god. Instead they added the figure of Satan to their cosmology. Satan could fill the Zoroastrian role of Angra Mainyu without threatening the purity of the Jews' cherished monotheism.

Satan did not appear within the Pentateuch, the Five Books of Moses. His absence in the Book of Genesis is particularly revealing as that book contained the mythology of the Jews, a mythopoeic account of the origins of the world and of the Jewish people.

The Catholic Church has long claimed that the serpent in the Garden of Eden was in fact Satan. But this claim makes no sense in the context of the story. The story of Adam and Eve was meant to explain a number issues which the ancient Jews found puzzling. Among these issues were menstruation, painful childbirth, female subservience, the snake's lack of limbs and the instinctive enmity between humans and snakes.

Rather than thinking of the snake's lack of limbs as an adaptation to allow them to more easily invade the burrows of their rodent prey, they chose to think of it as a divine curse. This was the reason why the snake had to appear in the Garden of Eden as a tempter, to justify the curse. Naturally, the snake had to be able to speak in order for it to fulfill its role in the story. Giving animals the power of human speech was not all that unusual in mythopoeic stories.

A Chinese mythopoeic story intended to explain both the three meals a day humans must eat and the subservience of the ox gave the ox the powers of speech for the sake of the story. In that story, the Celestial Emperor took pity on humans for having to work so hard to provide themselves with food every day. Therefore, he issued a proclamation that henceforth humans would only need to eat once every three days. The Celestial Emperor sent the ox to announce his proclamation but the ox misspoke and declared that the Celestial Emperor had decreed that humans would henceforth need to eat three times a day. The proclamation could not be changed and in order to help people as well as to punish the ox for his error, the Celestial Emperor decreed that the ox would henceforth serve as humanity's slave.

Satan's first real appearance in the Old Testament was the Book of Job. Here Satan plays the role of accuser

183

and goads God into taking everything from Job to find out how he would react. The real import of the book was to try to explain why evil befalls the righteous, though I have to admit that the book's explanation actually falls rather flat to my mind. Satan causes it in order to test the faith of the righteous.

By the time that the New Testament was written Satan had developed into a fallen angel who spreads lies and tempts men into sinning. By then Satan was also equated with Baalzebub, one of the gods worshipped by the Philistines. In the New Testament Satan is the chief of the fallen angels and the very personification of sin.

It is Satan who tempts Jesus in the desert and Satan who ensures that Judas Iscariot betrays Jesus. The Book of Revelations gives us the most complete view of Satan of any book of the Bible. In the near future Satan will send his son, the Antichrist to the world. Satan will gain control over the world and will be worshipped in place of God. This will lead to the final moral collapse of the human race and usher in the end of the world.

Jesus will return in glory. The angels will wage war against Satan and his army of demons. The angels will be victorious and Satan will be cast into hell. As Satan is the personification of sin his defeat and casting into hell represents the final victory of virtue over sin. Evil is finally destroyed and cast out of the world.

But the Bible was not the last word on either Satan or the nature of evil. This was hardly a surprise as Satan only really appeared in the Old Testament as a rather shadowy figure and in the New Testament only in the vaguest outline. It was inevitable that the figure of Satan would spark the imagination and spawn a whole literature to fill in the many blanks which the biblical canon left behind.

An interesting part of the process of filling in these blanks was the identification of Lucifer with Satan. The name, Lucifer, means "Bringer of Light" in Latin. Lucifer was originally a rather minor Roman god. He was the herald of Apollo and the Romans imagined him as a young man riding a horse. He was the personification of the morning star and as such he was believed to ride over the horizon just before dawn to announce the coming of the sun. There was no mythology attached to him which made it easier to conflate him with Satan.

This conflation began with the Latin translation of the Book of Isaiah. Isaiah 14:12 described the casting down of the morning star. Since the original Hebrew called the morning star the "son of the morning and the bringer of light" when it was translated into Latin the Hebrew word "helel" was translated as "Lucifer."

The passage is rather vague but seems to refer to the downfall of an earthly king rather than a supernatural being. Nevertheless, Christian readers came to believe that the passage predicted the downfall of Satan described in the Book of Revelation. It was this belief that caused the identification of Lucifer with Satan. Interestingly enough, Lucifer is far more famous as a synonym for Satan than he ever was as the herald of Apollo.

89) Slow News Day

I tend to become more philosophical in my thinking on days when Donald Trump doesn't do or say anything particularly foolish. The previous entry was primarily inspired by watching episodes of the eleventh season of *Supernatural*. Lucifer and God both figured prominently in those episodes. It just goes to show that I never know where my thoughts might lead and I never know what might inspire those thoughts. That's why I titled this book *Thoughts Out of Season*. There was no plan behind this

except to record and expound upon my thoughts as I have
them.

90) The Chicken and the Egg

It is perhaps one of the most famous conundrums,
"which came first, the chicken or the egg." At first blush it
seems like an unsolvable riddle since the chicken clearly
had to hatch from an egg while the egg just as clearly had
to be laid by a chicken. In reality the solution is
remarkably simple, the answer depends on whether you
believe in creationism or evolution as the explanation for
the existence of life.

For the creationist the chicken came first. The first
chicken was created out of thin air by God. Thus there
would have been no need for an egg.

For the evolutionist the egg came first. The first
chicken was the product of evolution, it evolved from
parents who were similar to chickens but not quite chickens.
Thus, the first chicken was hatched from an egg laid by a
bird who was closely related to the chicken but not quite a
chicken.

91) A Sad Dedication

I don't normally bother to read the dedications to the
books I read. The typical book is dedicated to someone
who was far more meaningful for the author of the book
than for the reader. To be perfectly honest, the fact that an
author has dedicated a book to his parents, his wife or his
kids is usually something of complete indifference to me. I
have never included a dedication in any of the books I have
published so far.

For some reason I made an exception for William Manchester's *The Arms of Krupp*. I don't recall why I read the dedication for that particular book. Most likely I caught a glimpse of it and immediately saw that it was not the typical dedication:

"For The children of Buschmannshof
Who lie at Voerde-bei-Dinslaken
And have no other monument."

The Arms of Krupp deals with the history of the Krupp family with a special emphasis on their steel making business from 1820 to 1967. The Krupp company originally manufactured wheels for trains and steel rails. Later, they expanded their product line to include steel barreled cannon. By the 1870's the company's main line of business was the manufacture and sale of artillery pieces and ship's armor. By the end of the 19th century the Krupp firm had become one of the largest manufacturers of armaments in the world.

During World War II the Krupp firm under the direction of Alfried Krupp supplied all branches of the German armed forces with weapons and armor. They were the principle armorer of the Third Reich.

Like most of the major industrial enterprises in Germany during World War II, the Krupp firm employed slave laborers conscripted from the countries conquered by the German army. They also employed concentration camp inmates from Dachau and Auschwitz. Krupp even maintained a factory within the Auschwitz-Birkenau complex.

But Krupp went beyond the other companies. The firm maintained its own concentration camps which it staffed with its own police. One of these company camps was located at Buschmannshof.

The Buschmannshof camp was a unique institution. Not only was it privately owned and operated but the prisoners interned there were all infants and toddlers who had been born to the slave laborers working in Krupp's Essen factories. It was a small camp with perhaps only a few hundred inmates. The treatment received by the prisoners at Buschmannshof was no better than the treatment received at any of the concentration camps operated by the SS. Malnutrition and disease were just as rampant at Buschmannshof as they were at the SS camps. The only real difference was that the prisoners who died at Buschmannshof were buried at Voerde-bei-Dinslaken, a tiny village near the camp.

The Buschmannshof camp was liquidated by the SS in March 1945. It just wouldn't do for British or American soldiers to stumble upon a concentration camp for infants and toddlers. The children in the camp were loaded into SS trucks and then were never seen or heard from again. It was not difficult to imagine what their fate was. None of the inmates from Buschmannshof survived the war.

So thorough was the effort to erase any trace of Buschmannshof that even many of the bodies buried at Voerde-bei-Dinslaken were disinterred and moved to other cemeteries. It just wouldn't do to have too many unidentified infants and toddlers buried together in a cemetery of a village as small as Voerde-bei-Dinslaken.

So William Manchester dedicated his book to the memory of the children interned at Buschmannshof. It was without a doubt the saddest dedication I have ever encountered.

92) United States Department of Education

The Department of Education was spun off from the Department of Health, Education and Welfare in 1980. The separation of Education into a separate department caused the Department of Health, Education and Welfare to be renamed the Department of Health and Human Services.

A Republican Representative from Kentucky, Thomas Massie, introduced a bill in the House of Representatives to abolish the United States Department of Education. The rationale behind the abolition was that education policy should be set at the state and local level rather than by bureaucrats in Washington. While that justification certainly seems well within the bounds of conservative thought, it does make me wonder. Does this mean that we can soon expect a repeal of the No Child Left Behind Act?

The timing of this bill is interesting as well. Why introduce it on the very day that Betsy DeVos was confirmed by the narrowest margin possible, a 51-50 vote that required Vice President Pence to cast the tie-breaking vote in order to consummate the confirmation?

The proposed bill only abolishes the department. It makes no provisions for who would administer federal student financial aid programs after the department is abolished. Perhaps the Republicans intend to eliminate those programs altogether? That, too, would be consistent with conservative dogma. But I don't imagine eliminating those programs would be too popular with voters, especially college students and their parents.

93) Khutulun

Khutulun was a Mongol princess who lived towards the end of the 13th century. She refused to marry any man who could not defeat her in wrestling. Those men who wrestled her and lost would be required to pay her 100 horses. She did eventually get married despite the fact that she had never been defeated in wrestling. She fell in love with the lucky man and did not require him to wrestle her. By then she had acquired a herd of 10,000 horses from her would-be suitors.

94) Black Robe

About two and a half years ago I watched a movie made in 1991 called *Black Robe*. It was about a Jesuit missionary sent to convert the Huron Indians in the 17th century.

In one memorable scene one of the Huron chiefs asked, "Do I get to have sex in heaven?"

The missionary answered, "No."

The chief then said, "Then why do I want to go?"

95) Small Pox

The champion killer of humanity was small pox. While black death and influenza certainly produced more spectacular pandemics, those pandemics only lasted a couple of years before dissipating. Small pox killed worldwide year after year. More Native Americans died from small pox than were killed by soldier's bullets. No one was immune to small pox. Even the crown heads of Europe succumbed to it.

It was the first disease for which a vaccination was developed. In fact, the very word, "vaccination," is derived from the Latin word, vacca, meaning "cow". in 1796 Dr. Edward Jenner published a paper demonstrating that people infected with cow pox were immune to small pox. He made this discovery when he investigated an old wives tale that milkmaids never caught small pox. Dr. Jenner's investigation verified that the legend was true because milkmaids were exposed to cow pox and infection with cow pox conferred immunity to small pox.

Once the greatest threat to human life, thanks to two hundred years of vaccination it has now been eradicated. There has not been a single documented case of small pox anywhere in the world in the last 36 years.

96) An Accident of Geography

It is well known that Christopher Columbus believed after studying the accounts of the travels of Marco Polo that he could sail from the west coast of Europe and reach India and China.

The financial rewards for establishing direct maritime trade with China and India were immense but Columbus lacked the wherewithal to finance the expedition himself. So he required the support of a wealthy patron.

Columbus first sought that support from the King of Portugal. He first approached the Portuguese court in 1485. King John II was not interested in backing Columbus' expedition for two reasons. The first was that the King's own experts regarded Columbus' proposal as impossible. The second was that Portugal was already secretly exploring the west coast of Africa in the hopes of discovering a sea route to India.

Columbus was persistent, however. He approached John II again in 1488. Again, Columbus failed to gain the

King's patronage. That year Bartholomew Dias had rounded the Cape of Good Hope, thus discovering the sea route to the Indian Ocean. The Portuguese King thus pinned his hopes on reaching India by circumnavigating Africa and then crossing the Indian Ocean.

After failing to win over the King of Portugal, Columbus returned to his native Italy and tried to find backing there. He approached both Venice and Genoa but both cities were already making money from the spice trade and had no wish to finance a transatlantic expedition.

Next, Columbus approached Their Catholic Majesties, the King and Queen of Spain. The Portuguese had not yet reached India, so Columbus was still hopeful that by sailing west he could beat the them to the punch. Columbus believed that India was much closer to Europe than it really was and that by sailing across the Atlantic he could reach it much sooner than the Portuguese could by circumnavigating Africa and then sailing eastwards.

While King Ferdinand and Queen Isabella were indeed impressed with Columbus' presentation, they knew that they lacked the knowledge to adequately judge its potential. Therefore, they sent Columbus to the University of Salamanca. If Columbus could convince the professors there that his proposal had merit then they would agree to finance the expedition.

In one of the most famous episodes in history, Columbus presented his proposal to the professors at Salamanca and they promptly laughed in his face. The faculty of the university did not believe that Columbus' proposal had any merit whatsoever. What he was proposing was patently impossible and therefore doomed to fail. The professors duly reported their conclusion to their King and Queen who, upon the advice of the professors, declined to patronize Columbus' endeavor.

Ferdinand and Isabella had a change of heart when they learned that Columbus would approach the Kings of

France and England if he could not gain their support. Ferdinand and Isabella agreed to pay Columbus an annual allowance if he would remain in Spain while they reconsidered his proposal. They also used the re-conquest of Spain as an excuse for not sending the expedition immediately.

By 1492 the Spaniards re-conquered Granada, the last Moorish bastion in Spain. With the re-conquest completed Ferdinand and Isabella no longer had any excuse for delaying the expedition further. They duly outfitted three ships for Columbus to use. The rest of the story is well known. Columbus sailed westward and encountered the Bahamas approximately where he had expected to find India. That was why he called the people "Indians" and the Native Americans have been stuck with the appellation ever since.

The part of the story that was usually misunderstood was the reason why the professors at Salamanca and the experts of King John II thought Columbus' proposal impossible.

Conventional wisdom held that the scholars in both Spain and Portugal still clung to the idea that the world was flat and believed that Columbus would sail off the edge of the world if he tried to reach India by sailing west from Europe. Thus, conventional wisdom portrayed Columbus as a visionary who correctly believed that the world was round while his detractors were foolish reactionaries who clung to the old myth of the flat earth.

This was not the case. Every educated person in 15th century Europe knew that the world was round. The roundness of the earth had been proven by the ancient Greek philosophers some two thousand years earlier. Experts in geography even knew the approximate size of the earth to a remarkably close degree. The circumference of the earth had already been computed by the Greek geographer Eratosthenes in the third century B.C. His approximation was off a little because he had naturally assumed that the earth formed a perfect sphere when in fact the earth bulges at the equator and is flattened somewhat at the poles.

The nature of the dispute between Columbus and the scholars was not over the shape of the earth but its size. Columbus believed that it was a third smaller than Eratosthenes' calculations indicated. That was why he believed that he could sail westward across the Atlantic and reach India. The scholars didn't think his proposal was impossible because he would fall off the edge of the world. They believed that it was impossible because he would run out of food and water long before he reached India or China.

The scholars were essentially correct. The only reason that Columbus did not in fact run out of food and water was because of the historical accident that the New World happened to lie exactly where he had expected to find India and China. Columbus made five expeditions and at no time was he ever within sight of either India or China.

97) Swallowing Pills

Ever since I underwent a partial glossectomy in April of 2012 to remove a cancer tumor my ability to swallow has been seriously impaired. So impaired, in fact, that I was diagnosed with dysphagia. Swallowing pills has sometimes proven to be a particular challenge for me.

Blood tests have shown that I have both type 2 diabetes and high cholesterol. I am currently taking medication to control both. I also have erectile dysfunction, probably a consequence of the diabetes, but since I am not currently in a romantic relationship I am not currently taking medication for it. I did take Cialis for a while and when I was taking it I did see a marked improvement in my erectile dysfunction but I did not have the opportunity to truly test the limits of that improvement.

Anyway, I currently take Atorvastatin to control my cholesterol and Metformin to control my blood sugar. Swallowing the Atorvastatin poses no problems since the pills are rather small. The Metformin, on the other hand, that is significantly larger. Large enough that swallowing can be a serious challenge.

Since a significant portion of my tongue is now composed of muscle tissue transplanted from my thigh and that new tissue has since been tethered to the floor of my mouth by scar tissue, I do not have normal mobility in my tongue. Also, my tongue is shaped very differently from a normal tongue. The combination of both of these features makes swallowing large pills like my Metformin tablets challenging and even potentially dangerous.

In order to have any hope of swallowing the Metformin tablets at all I must carefully place them on my tongue as close to the back and as close to the middle as possible.

If I do not place the pill far enough back, it will not go down into my throat. When this happens most of the time during the act of swallowing my tongue presses the pill against the roof of my mouth, thus preventing it from sliding into my throat. Often the pill becomes stuck to the roof of my mouth and I must then pry it loose with my fingers before I can try swallowing it again.

If I do not place it close enough to the center, it will roll off my tongue. When this happens the pill slides to the side of my mouth before rolling under the tongue. As I cannot lift my tongue, I have to fish the pill out with my fingers. This can be quite time consuming as well as being a rather uncomfortable experience.

The worst experience, however, is when the pill gets stuck in my throat. Most of the time it is simply a matter of drinking enough fluids to wash the pill down my throat. There have been times, however, when the pill went into my trachea rather than my esophagus.

When this happens I find myself choking on the pill. During the few times when this has happened I have never completely aspirated the pill. I have always managed to cough it back up. Nevertheless, it is a very uncomfortable and frightening experience. Not as bad as choking on food as I never felt that my life was actually in danger but still intensely unpleasant.

There have been a couple of times when the Metformin pill became lodged in my throat in such a way that no amount of fluid could flush it down. In these cases my body encases the pill in mucus.

I could feel the pill stuck in my throat. I would try to swallow to drive it down but to no avail. With the pill stuck in my throat swallowing would be much more difficult. When I tried to drink water to flush the pill down I would find that I could not swallow the water. The attempt at drinking would trigger a gag reflex which would in turn cause me to regurgitate the water.

I would find myself puking up the water I had just tried to swallow. This water would immediately be followed by a surprisingly enormous wad of mucus. Upon examination of this mucus I would find the Metformin pill embedded deep within the wad.

Such experiences have been mercifully rare. Still, sometimes I wonder if I should ask to receive my Metformin in liquid form rather than in pill form.

98) Trump's Cabinet

As Donald Trump's cabinet shapes up I am increasingly finding the whole process a bit unnerving. Trump, like Obama, ran on a platform of bringing fundamental change to the system. But when you look at Trump's cabinet level appointments, it doesn't seem like he is doing anything any differently than any of his predecessors, Obama included. His appointments are the same type of political paybacks that have been going on since nearly the founding of the republic.

Probably the only President who selected his cabinet solely on the basis of ability and qualifications was George Washington. But then again, Washington had the luxury of not being beholden to a political machine for his election to the presidency.

Looking at Trump's nominations one has to ask oneself, "Are these really the best people Trump could find?" In some cases the answer is probably "yes" but in other cases the answer is undeniably "no."

Trump's best choices were confirmed quickly with very little opposition. John Kelly was confirmed as Trump's Secretary of Homeland Security on inauguration day by a vote of 88-11. Thus he became the first cabinet member to be confirmed. Kelly was eminently qualified for the position. He was a retired four star Marine Corps general with a very distinguished service record.

Trump's nominee for Secretary of Defense, James Mattis, was also a retired four star Marine general with a service record as impressive as Kelly's. His confirmation vote was 98-1 and he, too, was confirmed on inauguration day.

Trump nominated Mike Pompeo for Director of the Central Intelligence Agency. Pompeo's confirmation was relatively fast. He was confirmed on January 23rd making him the third trump nominee to be confirmed by the full Senate. However, unlike his colleagues at Homeland Security and Defense, Pompeo's nomination did have significant opposition from the Democrats. His confirmation vote was 66-32. Pompeo was not completely without qualifications. His service on the House

Intelligence Committee certainly would have provided him with some background in intelligence matters but his lack of direct experience with espionage was probably the reason for the significant Democratic opposition.

Trump's next confirmed nominee was his choice for Ambassador to the United Nations, Nikki Haley. Her confirmation vote on January 24th was 96-4. I have to admit that I am confused about how she garnered a 96-4 vote. There is absolutely nothing in her background to suggest that she would make an effective ambassador. She has no experience in diplomacy whatsoever. Before her appointment, she had served as Governor of South Carolina and before that she served as a state representative.

On January 31st the Senate confirmed Trump's nominee for Secretary of Transportation, Elaine Chao, by a vote of 93-6. Ms. Chao had previously served as George Bush's Secretary of Labor. Given her experience and the non-controversial nature of her department, Ms. Chao seems an excellent choice. The Senate obviously agreed.

Rex Tillerson was confirmed as Secretary of State on February 1st by a vote of 56-43. Tillerson's entire career was spent as an executive for ExxonMobil. He has no diplomatic or government experience whatsoever. The irony is that while his career certainly provided him with experience in dealing with foreign governments that same experience also creates questions of conflict of interest. That experience notwithstanding, I do not believe that Tillerson is qualified to be the Secretary of State. Then again, I wasn't at all sure that either Hilary Clinton or John Kerry were qualified, either.

Now we come to Betsy DeVos, Trump's nominee for Secretary of Education. She has absolutely no background in educational theory, practice or policy. Her nomination was so obviously a political payoff that it couldn't have been anything else. Her only qualification seems to be her status as a major donor to the Republican

Party and its candidates, including some of those who voted on her confirmation. Her confirmation vote on February 7th was 51-50. She owes her confirmation to Vice President Pence's tie-breaking vote.

DeVos's confirmation illustrates the biggest problem facing our country. The vote was almost strictly along party lines with two Republicans voting against her confirmation. The fact that so many Republicans would vote to confirm a nominee as patently unqualified as DeVos proves that party loyalty is more important to politicians than the national interest.

The whole purpose for Senate confirmation of presidential appointments is to provide a check to presidential authority and to ensure that those appointed are actually qualified for office. The Republican senators who voted to confirm DeVos clearly abdicated their constitutional responsibilities for the sake of party loyalty. February 7th was a sad day for the republic.

Tom Price was confirmed by the Senate as Secretary of Health and Human Services on February 10th. The vote was again completely along party lines, 52-47. While Price is certainly qualified to administer Health and Human Services, he was an orthopedic surgeon before entering into a political career, he was perceived by Democrats as too much of a conservative ideologue for the position.

Steven Mnuchin's confirmation hearing is scheduled for February 11th, the day after this writing. Mnuchin is Trump's nominee for Secretary of the Treasury. Mnuchin is a hedge fund manager who was once a partner at Goldman Sachs. Placing him in charge of the Treasury Department would also put him in charge of the Securities and Exchange Commission and the Internal Revenue Service. Seems to me that this would be tantamount to putting the fox in charge of inspecting the henhouse. But then again, that has been done before. After all, the first

Commissioner of the Securities and Exchange Commission had been Joseph Kennedy, Sr., a man who had augmented his fortune through insider trading.

Representative Ryan Zinke is Trump's nominee for Secretary of the Interior. While he has some limited experience in the House of Representatives and the Montana State Senate, there really isn't anything in his background that makes him especially qualified to be the next Secretary of the Interior. His confirmation hearing has not been scheduled yet.

Trump's nominee for Secretary of Agriculture is Sonny Purdue. He was a veterinarian and small business owner before serving in the Georgia Senate and then as Governor of Georgia. Nothing in his background even suggests any particular expertise with agriculture, however. His nomination has not yet been reviewed by any Senate committees and his confirmation hearing has not yet been scheduled.

Trump nominated Wilbur Ross for Secretary of Commerce. A billionaire like Trump himself, it is tempting the dismiss Ross as another Trump crony or a man who bought his nomination. But Ross made his fortune by buying failing companies, turning them around and then selling them at a substantial profit. Sounds to me like the kind of man needed to run the Commerce Department. His confirmation hearing has not yet been scheduled but I would not expect him to have much difficulty winning the nomination.

Andrew Puzder is certainly a controversial choice for Secretary of Labor. Puzder is a fast food company executive and all fast food companies thrive by underpaying and exploiting their employees. Puzder was also a financial contributor to Trump's election campaign. Nothing about his background qualifies him to be Secretary of Labor. On the contrary, his experience as a fast food company executive should actually be a disqualification. I expect his confirmation hearing to be long and tendentious. I expect him to be confirmed but Pence might have to cast the tie-breaking vote again to make it happen.

Ben Carson seems an odd choice to head the Department of Housing and Urban Development. As a pediatric neurosurgeon Carson was one of the best in the world but how exactly does that qualify him to head a department concerned primarily with urban planning? I would think that he would have been far better qualified to be Secretary of Health and Human Services. He probably would have been less controversial than Price. His confirmation hearing has not yet been scheduled.

Trump's nominee for Secretary of Energy is former Governor of Texas, Rick Perry. While there is nothing in Perry's background to suggest that he has any special expertise in energy policy, he did serve as Governor of Texas for fourteen years. Obviously energy policy would be important to the economy of Texas as it is a major producer of domestic crude oil. So I would hope that Perry would have learned quite a bit about energy policy during his tenure. Nevertheless, I think Trump could have easily found a more qualified candidate. In fact, I think that Tillerson is probably far better qualified to be Energy Secretary than Perry, or for that matter, better qualified to be Energy Secretary than Secretary of State. Then again, Tillerson's background as an oil company executive would certainly have raised questions of conflict of interest had he been nominated as Secretary of Energy.

David Shulkin is an interesting choice for Secretary of Veteran Affairs as he is the current Undersecretary of Veteran Affairs for Health. He has served in this position for the last year and a half after being appointed by President Barack Obama. That's right, Trump actually kept someone from the outgoing Obama administration. Shulkin's confirmation hearing is scheduled for February 13th. I expect him to be confirmed easily.

Trump has nominated Oklahoma Attorney General Scott Pruitt as his Administrator of the Environmental Protection Agency. Pruitt has claimed that the scientific community is divided on the issue of global warming. During his career as a lawyer and as Attorney General of Oklahoma he has sued the Environmental Protection Agency repeatedly. In fact, he even described himself on his own website as "a leading advocate against the EPA's activist agenda." I think that alone should completely disqualify him from the position as head of the EPA.

Confirming Pruitt as head of the EPA would not be like putting the fox in charge of the henhouse, it would be like putting a man in charge of the henhouse who advocates the extermination of chickens. Pruitt's confirmation hearing has not yet been scheduled. It will be interesting to see if the Republican Party possesses enough party discipline to ram this obviously inappropriate nomination through the full Senate.

Robert Lighthizer is Donald Trump's nominee for United States Trade Representative. Lighthizer is a lawyer with extensive experience as a trade negotiator, including serving as Deputy Trade Representative during the Reagan Administration. Lighthizer is very well qualified and should easily win confirmation. His confirmation hearing has not yet been scheduled.

Trump's choice to be the next Director of the Office of Management and Budget is Mick Mulvaney. I don't see anything about Mulvaney's background to suggest that he is even qualified for the position. His education is significant. He has earned degrees in International Economics, Commerce and Finance from Georgetown University and a Doctor of Law degree from the University of North Carolina at Chapel Hill. While certainly impressive, I don't see how they qualify him to direct the Office of Management and Budget. Business disciplines are not interchangeable. The Office of Management and Budget is involved with the intricate accounting of the executive branch. It should be headed by a person with a substantial background in government accounting. The disciplines of economics and finance are simply not relevant to the operation of the Office of Management and Budget. Mulvaney's legislative experience is interesting, he has served in the South Carolina House of Representatives, the South Carolina Senate and the United States House of Representatives. But again it is no more relevant than his educational background. Seems to me that he could have been nominated for a post that would be a better fit for his background. Mulvaney's confirmation hearing has not been scheduled yet.

Trump's choice for Administrator of the Small Business Administration should not generate much controversy. Who would complain about nominating a very successful business woman to head the agency intended to promote small business? Just because that business involves professional wrestling doesn't make her accomplishments any less impressive. I would expect Linda McMahon to easily win confirmation.

Dan Coats is Trump's nominee for Director of National Intelligence. Coats has served in the United States Senate for sixteen years and the United States House of Representatives for eight years. He also served as Ambassador to Germany for three and a half years. During his tenure in the Senate Coats was a member of the Select Committee on Intelligence. I do wonder if that by itself is adequate preparation for the job. Wouldn't it be better to have someone with actual espionage experience? Still, Coats is better qualified than many of Trump's other nominees. Nevertheless, I cannot help but have the feeling that Coats would have made a better Secretary of State, especially considering Tillerson's lack of credentials in diplomacy. Could Coats be yet another example of candidate nominated for the wrong job?

99) Snow Days

When I was a kid way back in the Dark Ages, school wouldn't close unless there was at least three or four inches of snow on the ground. For a couple of inches school might be delayed for an hour or two. But I can't remember there ever being a day when school was even delayed by a snowfall of less than an inch.

On February 9th the schools here in Chambersburg were closed because of inclement weather. The next day they opened two hours late. Given my own experiences from when I was in school, I would have expected nothing short of a major snow storm to close schools one day and delay their opening on the next. At least half a foot of snowfall if not a full foot.

While Chambersburg certainly does not get the amount of snowfall seen in some parts of the country, six inches is not all that unusual over here. The first winter I spent in Chambersburg we got a couple of feet one day.

Now, it did indeed snow on the morning of February 9th. But the snowfall couldn't have amounted to a full inch. Granted, I didn't actually go outside and measure the snow but when I looked out the window it sure didn't look like much deeper than half an inch. I couldn't believe that the Board of Education had actually closed schools because of it. I was even more surprised when I learned that schools were under a two hour delay the next morning. Especially when there was no additional snowfall in the meantime.

After performing a Google search I was able to find the official snowfall for Chambersburg from the National Weather Service. Chambersburg received between one and two inches of snow. Deeper than I expected but still it hardly seemed like enough to cancel school for a day, much less delay school openings the next day.

Of course, the situation could have been worse. One time I was flying to London and Heathrow Airport was closed due to snowfall. My plane landed at Cardiff instead.

As Cardiff did not normally receive intercontinental flights their customs and passport control personnel were inadequate to handle the number of passengers carried by a transatlantic flight.

The British Airport Authority provided buses that took us from Cardiff to London. The buses dropped us off at Heathrow. From there I had to take another shuttle bus as the above ground sections of the London Underground were shut down by the snow as well.

The second shuttle took us to the nearest below ground station. From there I was able to ride the Underground into Central London.

When I arrived in Central London I found that very little was open. It seemed that the whole city shut down because of the unexpected snowfall. How much snow did London get? Only a quarter of an inch. A quarter of an inch was enough to shut down one of the largest cities in Europe. Well, that was my impression of the depth of the snow. I could be wrong. It might have even been a full inch in depth, perhaps even an inch and a half, like in Chambersburg. So, Chambersburg should not feel bad for closing their schools. At least most of the businesses stayed open which is more than I could say for London.

100) Movies

I have become quite the movie aficionado in recent years. It all started when I subscribed to Netflix on June 24, 2012. At the time I was not working and still undergoing radiation therapy and chemotherapy for my cancer.

I had always enjoyed watching movies. Most of the movies I had seen in my life I had watched on television. I only on rare occasions actually watched a movie in a theater. But for most of my life I was only an occasional watcher. I typically might watch one or two movies in a month.

I remember that when my family first subscribed to HBO in 1982 I had watched movies quite a bit more frequently. I guess it was the novelty of being able to see a movie shortly after its theatrical release and also being able to see it uncut and uninterrupted. I don't know how many movies I watched during the first year or two but I am sure that it was a substantial number, probably two or three a week. Eventually, the novelty of HBO wore off and the frequency with which I watched movies steadily diminished.

Since I started subscribing to Netflix I have watched movies just about every day. I both stream movies and I rent DVDs through the mail. My subscription is set at the maximum number of DVDs available, three at a time. Still, I stream probably 50 or 60 movies for every DVD I rent. I try to watch at least one movie every day. Often I watch more than one. There have been entire days when I watched as many movies as possible. My current record is eight for a single day.

I watch all kinds of movies, both foreign and domestic. I watch old classics as well as the latest releases. The oldest movie I've watched is *Le Voyage Dans le Lune* made in 1902. That movie may well have been the first movie adaptation of a novel. I know this because I also happen to have read the novel from which it was derived, H.G. Wells' *The First Men in the Moon*.

As of this writing I have watched 3879 movies. I know this so exactly because I have compiled a list of them. I suspect that by now the only people who have seen more movies than I have are professional movie critics.

The interesting thing is that I do not remember the vast majority of the movies I have seen. In fact, if I hadn't maintained a list of them I would not be able to tell you which movies I have seen and which I have not. Naturally, this brings up the question of the futility of the whole exercise. It begs the question, "If you don't even remember most of the movies you have watched, then what is the point of watching them at all?"

Well, the point is passing the time. The point is that you never know how much you will enjoy a movie until after you have watched it. And while I don't remember the vast majority of the movies I have watched, I do remember the ones worth remembering. So, while most of the movies I watch are completely forgettable there are those rare few that do provide lifelong memories. Ultimately, it is those movies that make the whole undertaking worthwhile.

I have never regretted watching a movie no matter how bad that movie may have proven to be. After all, it is only by experiencing truly bad movies that you can really appreciate the truly great ones. I used to think that such stars as Arnold Schwarzenegger and John Wayne were bad actors until I watched some of the truly horrible acting in some of the worst movies ever made. Even delivering lines in a normal tone of voice requires some talent. Talent which most of us do not have.

Of course the greatest actors have incredible range. They can play anyone or anything convincingly. John Wayne did an excellent job as an actor so long as he did not stray from within the narrow range which his limited talents allowed. But within that range he was probably as effective an actor as anyone else. The same can be said of Sylvester Stallone and Arnold Schwarzenegger. Not everyone can be Laurence Olivier and we should not wish everyone to be. After all, it would be hard to appreciate the monumental talent of an actor like Olivier if there were not for the performance of inferior actors for comparison.

Sometimes I find inspiration in movies. I have been inspired with more than one plot for a novel after watching a movie. This happened when I watched *The Devil and Daniel Webster*. It happened again when I watched *Goosebumps*. The fact that I have not yet gotten around to finishing either of those manuscripts doesn't diminish in my mind the importance of seeing those two movies. And that to my mind is another justification for watching them. In the end a movie is simply another medium for telling a story. So watching movies can be every bit as important and inspirational to the author as reading books.

Index